Dream Big

Ninety-Nine Steps to Network Marketing Success

By

Doug Wead
and
Joshua Wead

Introduction:

Everything You Need to Succeed

Doug Wead, a former White House staffer and an adviser to two American presidents, is best known for his New York Times bestselling books on presidential history. His third son, Joshua, is a theology student at Southeastern University. What isn't known is that the two, father and son, have had a lifetime fascination with Network Marketing. What makes it work? Why does it work for some and not others?

This interest has taken them both across the world to six continents. They have interviewed the most successful and most controversial network marketers in the world. They have flown in their private jets, lunched on their yachts, and sat in the Green Room with them backstage. Always they have asked the same questions. What are the secrets to success in Network Marketing? What would you do differently if you started over? What do you teach your leaders?

Doug brings to this study a wealth of experience. Since 1974 when he was first invited to the stage by Dexter Yager in Charlotte, North Carolina, he has been one of the most popular speakers on the circuit sharing the stage with Ronald Reagan, Charlie "Tremendous" Jones, Zig Ziglar, Bob Proctor, Mark Victor Hansen and all the other great speakers on the circuit.

But Wead was more than a speaker. He was a listener. And he was a writer. Before Doug Wead there were no books in the famous "System," the program that brought training to Network Marketing and later brought wealth to its leaders. Wead changed all that. Just as he had written books for and with presidents, he became the ghostwriter for a generation of Network Marketing leaders, the man behind all of Dexter Yager's early books.

He has given a thousand speeches in most of the major soccer stadiums and coliseums of the world filling the largest auditoriums in North America, South America, Europe, Australia, Asia and Africa, and filling them ten or fifteen times with annual visits. Crowds have sometimes numbers in the 100,000 range. And on these international tours he helped build Network

21 from a small gathering of 250 people into an organization of millions.

Joshua was sometimes along on these trips. Watching and listening and learning for himself. When he reached his college years his interest in Network Marketing became a great curiosity. What is it? How do they make their money? Why is it so elusive for some and seemingly easy for others?

Joshua plays an invaluable role in this project. He brings to this study the questions, the innocence and the challenges of the person new to Network Marketing. He holds his father to the difficult task of explaining himself and of defining terms. Without Joshua, this book would have little practical use for a person new to networking.

Together they bring the long list of the most important principles and steps to Network Marketing success. To their knowledge, they have never been fully defined before. Most network marketers will tell you that they have tried "believing" and tried "persistence" and tried "qualifying prospects" and most have come away wondering what missing piece is still slowing the process down.

Others have blamed themselves, concluding that they are at fault and that the successful ones have some quality that they are lacking. The successful ones cannot be ordinary people. They have some built in advantage. And indeed, as explained in this book, there are times when some have stolen a group or transferred it, thus stealing the work of another. But even then, someone, somewhere, originally built that network.

This book breaks new ground in touching on the ethics of Network Marketing. And not in some arbitrary fashion. But rather in the practical sense. If you say or do this, what will be the consequences? And what will work better and why?

As both authors point out, no one can take all of these steps. No one will perfectly obey all of these rules or act on the principles. They will do some and neglect or fail in the others. And one can certainly be very successful without legalistically obeying these rules. But they will surely speed the process and ease the pain and save on investment expense.

These are principles that appear on one side or the other of an accountant's ledger. If you aren't doing them, they are on the negative side and it will take more work and money and time to build your network. If you are doing them, they will be on the positive side, inching you toward success. It is up to you to move as many of them to the positive side of the ledger as you can. Why argue with something that works. If it is in your power to do it, then get it done and with these steps see your dreams come true.

Dream Big

Ninety-Nine Steps to Network Marketing Success

1 - The importance of a dream.
2 - Share your dream with people you love.
3- Get counsel before you do anything in the business.
4- Listen to 5 recommended CDs.
5- Make a list of prospects.
6- Double your list of prospects.
7- Team up with someone else.
8- Practice setting up meetings with your prospects and your team.
9- Promote your upline team.
10- Don't call all of your prospects at once.
11- If involving a married couple, invite both the husband and wife.
12- Get into a Network Marketing educational system.
13- Read positive books.
14- Practice showing the plan.
15- Get some friends to see you rehearse the showing of the plan.
16- Audit other presentations.
17- Start a meeting in your own home.

18- Get the meeting out of your home.
19- Get a new face into your group.
20- Make sure the new face is loyal to you.
21- Have someone else introduce you at the meeting.
22- Develop your own signature.
23- Listen to a positive CD before showing the plan.
24- Have your upline teach your downline what they need to know.
25- Look successful.
26- Learn how to do one-on-ones.
27- Give a prospect a unique reason to get into your business.
28- Sponsor your weakness.
29- Calibrate your prospecting approach.
30- Sponsor peer and above.
31- Teach all of the networking principles, not just the ones that work for you.
32- Learn to teach how to lead rather than how to build.
33- Know when to take charge.
34- Follow up within the first 48 hours and never wait more than three days.
35- Use your products.
36- Talk about your products.
37- Categorize your new distributors as business builders or product people.
38- Revisit distributors in the business-product categories.
39- Never let a prospect get away without a referral.

40- Help your new distributor make a list.
41- Rehearse the invitation with your new distributor.
42- Remember, you are responsible for everything.
43- Set long term and short term goals.
44- Develop good work habits.
45- Get into a good field-oriented educational system.
46- Think of CD's as your employees, put them to work.
47- Build a CD library.
48- Lead by example.
49- Go to the functions.
50- Promote the functions.
51- Take your distributors with you to the functions.
52- Understand the dangers of crosslining.
53- Pass negative upline. Pass positive downline.
54- When you have no upline mentor, create one yourself.
55- Remember, people will work for recognition or money.
56- Promote your system.
57- Help your downline set networking goals.
58- Teach your downline how to promote.
59- Teach others how to promote you.
60- It's not what your upline does for you that will make you rich, but rather, what you do for your upline.

61- Understanding the importance of momentum.
62- Keep in mind that it is hard to build more than three separate groups at the same time.
63- Sponsor fifteen to twenty to find your three.
64- Don't decide on leaders too quickly.
65- Get help in launching an out of town group.
66- Make your prospect build locally before launching an out of town group.
67- Plan on making four weekly trips to launch an out of town group.
68- Plan on making a monthly trip for one year.
69- Visit your large groups at least once a year.
70- Back up a distributor with a distributor.
71- Back up a leader with a leader.
72- Back up a city with a city.
73- Back up a culture with a culture.
74- Back up a country with a country.
75- Spend less than you make.
76- Don't quit your job too quickly.
77- Keep out of debt and don't let your downline run up a big debt.
78- Invest in yourself.
79- Keep a check on your vital signs.
80- Understand the economic whiplash, or the six month delay.
81- Be patient, some things take time.
82- Be flexible.

83- Give your distributors everything they need to know to be successful.
84- Keep in mind you are in a business, not a charity.
85- Remember, what gets rewarded, gets duplicated.
86- Work with your strongest group.
87- Do a business review with your downline.
88- Learn to be an effective counselor.
89- Respect the opposite sex.
90- Never make a recommendation until you have heard both sides of a dispute.
91- Keep your upline mentor informed. There should be no surprises.
92- Always defer counseling and recognition to the higher leader.
93- Reward numbers as well as level of achievement.
94- Use healthy competition to build your network.
95- Don't prejudge prospects or leaders.
96- Be a good broker and learn to sponsor wholesale.
97- Stay focused.
98- Loyal leaders come through relationships.
99- Make a decision.

Step 1

The importance of a dream.

The first step in building a successful Network Marketing business is to visualize your success. To dream about it, to think it through. What would happen? How would it happen? What would I do with my success?

We interviewed more than 300 networking leaders from 30 different businesses and almost all of them agreed that this was the single most important step. And yet most people won't take the time.

Centuries ago Aristotle wrote about the relationship between "purpose" and "action" but the first observable and experiential studies began with Cecil Mace in 1935 and later more extensively by Edwin Locke in the 1960's. Locke was able to actually measure the difference between goal setters and the rest of us. The results were very impressive.

You'll encounter people who will tell you that they cannot build a networking business because they don't have any money, or they don't have any education, they are new in the city and they have no contacts. They'll give you a long list of reasons why they can't build a business but none of those prevent them from dreaming.

You don't have to have money to dream. You don't have to live in a certain town or have contacts to dream. Nothing stops you from dreaming. So if people who are successful say that the first step toward success is to visualize that success, why would we argue with something so simple? Let's find another rule to break, one that's a little more difficult. This one is easy, it's a no-brainer. Why would you wake up in the morning and tie your hand behind your back? Why would you do that? So you can say, "I built my business with one hand tied behind my back. I did it without a dream. And I employed none of that visualization stuff. No dream, nada."

But why? What have you achieved? If the first step closer is that easy and it costs no money and you don't have to experience rejection, then it is a step you should take.

Step 2

Share your dream with people you love.

When you share your dream with someone you love you will accomplish a number of things. First, they may help you achieve it. I remember a young cousin who announced to everybody that he was collecting stamps. He started getting stamps from uncles and aunts and grandparents and their friends. The stamps started coming from all over the world and as the years passed they never stopped. What about the other cousins? Why didn't I get gifts? Why didn't anyone remember me? Why him? Because he shared his dream.

Second, when you share your dream with someone you love they will likely be more understanding. If your children know why you are online or on the telephone or at a meeting they are more likely to understand if they know your goals.

One leader sat all of his family down and laid out his plan and told and stated some goals. When we hit this level, we are all going to Disneyland, so help me, cooperate. The family would push him out the door.

A business goal is less likely to be the cause of a misunderstanding in a relationship if the goal is distinctly established and each person reassured of their love. After all, the reason you are building a business is to make life better for your friends, too.

There is also a dark side to this principle. Never share your dreams with someone untrustworthy or someone who hates you or sees you as a rival. They will do everything they can to stop you even if it hurts themselves.

Remember the playroom when you first encountered other children? If you wanted the red truck there was always a bully who wanted it, too. When you chose the blue truck he dropped the red one and took that one. It turned out that he didn't really want either truck at all; he wanted to dominate you.

This process never stops and it is why you only carefully share your dreams with loved ones. Don't announce it from stage. If people know what you want, they won't let you have it.

From 1985-1988, I worked for the presidential campaign of George H. W. Bush. He brought on a very talented political adviser to run things named Lee Atwater. Hollywood made a movie about him starring Richard Gere. Flying on the campaign plane,

I had times to talk with the brilliant young Mr. Atwater and learn from him. He kept two books prominently positioned on his desk, *The Prince* by Machiavelli and *The Art of War* by Sun Tzu.

People would often ask him what he wanted to do if his candidate were elected president. Did he want to be his White House Chief of Staff? Power? Or run the Republican Party as its new Chairman? Most assumed he wanted the latter because he would not be serving in government and would be able to make millions of dollars on outside, private work as well. Power AND money.

But Lee Atwater was very circumspect and humble. "I only want the candidate to win." But he added, knowing that it was better to say something, "Well, I have this dream of helping to elect a head of state on three different continents. North America, Europe and South America." It was a diversion but it kept inquisitive people happy.

When George H. W. Bush won the election the competition was on to be the new Chairman of the Republican National Committee. There were two giants in the contest.

On the one hand was Rich Bond. He had been the President Elect's national political director. Most thought he would be fired after we lost the Iowa Caucus early in the contest. But Lee Atwater had insisted that he stay on. And Bond had done superbly.

But Rich Bond had some stiff competition from the multi-millionaire Fred Malek, CEO of the Marriot Corporation. He had charged nothing to come in and help run the campaign and he had brought a lot of talented people with him.

In those heady months something interesting unfolded in quick succession. *The Washington Post* ran a story suggesting that at President Nixon's behest Malek had once made a list of important Jewish officials serving at one of the federal agencies. Malek was suddenly out of the running. And then came the rumor, later proven false, that Rich Bond was the source of the story. Rich bond was out, too. Lee Atwater was named the new Chairman of the Republic National Committee. It was the job he had wanted all along. But he was smart enough not to let anyone know.

Don't share your dreams unless they are with people who love you and will work with you and will help you build your business together because most people, even friends and relatives, will oppose you when they see where you are headed. They will stop you. So, don't announce what you're going to do and how you're going to do it to everybody. First find the people who love you and team up with them. Share your dream with them so they know the sacrifices you will all be making and how you will build your business together.

Step 3

Get counsel before you do anything in the business.

It is important to get as much advice as possible before launching a networking business and there are a couple of reasons for that. First, the patterns you set now will be duplicated for good or bad as your network grows. You won't find it easy to correct the mistakes when your network is already growing exponentially. You will have to live with the consequences and some will be costly.

Second, you will immediately be working with your best friends and your best contacts. You will be picking the low hanging fruit. Your work of recruiting or sponsoring new distributors will get more complex, not easier. So you don't want to ruin your start.

Now, let's make one thing clear. Some networking leaders run their organizations with a strong hand. You don't want to join a "cult." You don't need the person who is bringing you into the networking company to be your "upline guru" who tells you whether you should get married in February or March. Someone who decides whether you should have two children or one. This is your independent business. You run this business. There should be no "upline guru" who tells you what to do. You tell yourself what to do.

But by the same token, your upline leaders in a given network have failed more than you have. They've spent more money and more time working the network than you. And every company and every situation is slightly different. So if you want to save money and save time you would be wise to ask for their advice. Get as much information as you can. And not just from your upline. Take advantage of the Internet to see what strategies others employ and why.

A word of caution: Every network organization within a company has unique problems and opportunities that are all its own. When you do your own independent research, take it to your upline to get their advice.

You don't have to take this advice. You are your own boss. But you would be foolish indeed not to hear them out. Their success depends on your success.

Many times we have sponsored a new person and been tempted to turn them loose to go to work. But usually we are smart enough to hold them back, to encourage them to study a little bit, to think things through before they act. Sometimes just one week of preparation will make all the difference in the world.

So get counsel before you or your people do anything in a networking business. Don't waste time that someone else has already spent. Don't waste money that someone else has already invested.

Step 4

Listen to 5 recommended CDs.

The key to success at anything is experience. The problem is that most successful people will not share their secrets. And why should they? Oh, they will share generic principles of hard work or goal setting. They will even write books about such platitudes. But they will avoid getting into the specifics of what really happened to bring success. They will always hold something back, something they see as proprietary. If they give it up it is like taking good right out of their children's mouths. That hard earned information is private. It has value. And it should be passed on carefully like an inheritance.

Network Marketing is totally different. In Network Marketing, a person's success depends on the growth and success of the distributors they sponsor. A good leader learns what works and then gets the information out as quickly as possible. And while certain basic rules remain fixed, such as the "steps" we are taking in this book, there are many nuances to building a network business. Some things depend on the country, the company, the products involved. And those nuances are everything.

You don't want to get into a network that doesn't have a good support system to help you grow. And if they have a good support system, they have CD's with stories of successful distributors. Get those CD's. Buy them. Borrow them. Listen to them. Learn from them. It is the closest thing to personal experience that you can get. It will help you plan and pace your own growth in Network Marketing. In the long run, it will save you a lot of time and a lot of money.

Step 5

Make a list of prospects.

This is a very obvious assignment but many people resist it out of stubbornness. They think it is an insult to their intelligence. Or maybe, subconsciously, they are afraid to take such a bold step. To put a name down on paper forces them to think about recruiting and they hate that because of their great fear of rejection.

Do it. No excuses.

We use different parts of our brain to see and to write and to speak. Making a written list of prospects for your Network Marketing business just makes good sense. Something happens when you make such a list. Just the act of writing a name down on paper puts your subconscious to work, thinking and reasoning about what you will say and how you will say it to recruit them into your network. You will even be working as you sleep.

In many parts of the world, your Facebook list of friends will be your prospect list. In Russia it will be Kontakte. Or you can manually create the list from all the people you work with or know.

Remember, we are working toward thousands of dollars in monthly income. There are some unpleasant things we have to do and recruiting is the big one. You increase your odds of success greatly in networking by making a list. Why have the odds working against you? So get on with it.

Step 6

Double your list of prospects.

When I was appointed to Senior Staff at the White House, the FBI came by my office and asked for a list of hundred people who knew me. I was flabbergasted. I said, "I don't know a hundred people. I can't get you a hundred people."

The agent was very kind and patient. "Yes you can," he stated very calmly. "You start making a list. You'll see. Everybody does it. You can do it. We want to know one hundred people you know."

Then, they wanted to know someone who lived on the same block with me every year of my life. I said, "That's impossible! I lived in Indianapolis, and then we moved to South Bend; we were in Terre Haute before that, I was three years old. How am I going to find someone who lived on the same block with me every year of my life even when I was just a little kid?"

The agent smiled. I was on his turf. He understood how this worked. "Yes, you can," he said calmly. "Everybody does it. You'll be surprised that you'll be able to do it."

And sure enough, he came back around days later and somehow, someway, I had it done. I had my one hundred names.

"This is very good," he smiled. But a week later he was back.

"Sorry to bother you, Mr. Wead," he said kindly. "You know that list of a hundred names you got us?"

"Yeah."

"Well, we need another hundred names."

"You've got to be kidding me. I can't come up with another hundred names." But I did. And you can, too.

Make your list of prospects. And when you feel you've done your best? Double it.

Step 7

Team up with someone else.

As you will learn later on, it is important for you to be part of a systematic approach to building your networking business. And it is usually more effective if you do not present the business opportunity yourself. No matter how important or credible you may be, you cannot be an authority on a business you just joined. And your friends will know that. You will want to have a Network Marketing mentor or partner or team member or upline leader do the work. Your job will be to get on the phone or online and set the meeting up.

If the person who sponsored you won't help you, ask them for their upline's contact information. And keep going upline until you find someone who is willing to work with you and help build your business.

Believe me, up there somewhere is a very talented leader looking for distributors who are serious about building a network and making money. They will be just as glad to find you as you will be to find them.

A number of years ago I was invited to Brisbane, Australia to speak for one of the most talented and successful network marketers in the world. He had massive groups in Indonesia, Hungary, Russia, South Africa and all over the world. I had spoken for soccer stadiums full of his people in Jakarta and Surabaya and Budapest. Now, I was going back to the source of it all, the group he had launched in Australia that had taken his network to the world.

What I found didn't surprise me. His home group was just a few hundred people. At one point I asked him what his group needed to hear. What teaching would be most effective? And then he opened up to me. He seemed to have no respect in his own group. No one wanted to work. He offered himself as a mentor and a team partner to help build larger groups in Australia and there wasn't a single person who would take him up on it.

Here was a millionaire, a young genius at networking, willing to give his time and energy free of charge and there was no one in his group who seemed to want it.

If you are new to Network Marketing, I can assure you that somewhere up there is a mentor ready to go to work to build your business. Find that person and team up. The

Chinese have a proverb: If you want to go fast? Go alone. If you want to go far? Take someone with you.

Plan on going far.

Step 8

Practice setting up meetings with your prospects and your team.

An old football coach once said, "It is not the will to win but the will to prepare to win that makes the difference."

You may be very clever and a very good conversationalist, but how you set up the meeting with the person showing the plan is critical. You will be setting a pattern that will be duplicated many times over and may be the key to success or failure as a network marketer. So practice what you will say.

Practice with the person who will be giving the presentation, whether it will be a one-on-one meeting or a gathering at a hotel.

There are three things to keep in mind about setting up a meeting or anything else you say to a prospect.

1.) It should be true. There is no reason to "trick" someone into getting into your business. If you are in a legitimate networking company that doesn't "frontload" or require a large investment to join, then you make little or no money for recruiting. You only make money when your prospect eventually makes money and then a small percent of their income. So why would anyone be dishonest or manipulative?

2.) It should be you. That is, you want to say things that are comfortable, that you believe, that do not violate your personality and who you are. If you wear a pair of shoes and they are uncomfortable, then no matter how good they look you will eventually grow tired of wearing them. And you want to find a way to talk to people that is comfortable for you.

3.) It has to work. If no one is responding to your invitations, stop. Go no further. Get advice from a networking leader in your company and find out what you can change to make your invite more effective.

Step 9

Promote your upline team.

The key to setting up meetings is how you promote the person who will be showing the business opportunity. This should be someone in your upline, someone who will also make money if your ventures are successful. This is how you can be sure that they will say and do the right things. It is in their interest, as well as yours, for the relationship to work and for the meetings to be effective.

Sometimes this person will be your direct upline. It is important for you to show loyalty and respect to your upline. Because how you treat them is how your own network will treat you. If your upline is uncouth and lazy or irresponsible, and you show respect to them anyway, it will be very hard for your own downline to be disloyal to you. After all, you were loyal in difficult circumstances.

So how do you promote the person who will be making the presentation? Ask them. And if they don't have an easy way for you to promote them, interview them and find positive things you can say about them.

If they are a hard worker, even an uneducated, old, poor upline can be promoted successfully. Even if they have no credentials or credibility, you can say, "This person is a legend in networking. They are the hardest workers in the business. If they take you on and agree to help you, then you will be very lucky indeed." Treat them with honor. Give them the best seat. Show deference to them. And your prospects, picking up on your attitude, will feel lucky to have their help.

It is usually important for you to promote more than one person upline. Don't put all of your eggs in one basket. If you have more than one hero in your upline team, then you increase the opportunities and you are not at the mercy of just one leader.

Step 10

Don't call all of your prospects at once.

Many people will launch into a new business and right away tell everyone they know. Sometimes their enthusiasm is contagious and there is growth. But usually they just ruin all of their best prospects.

Not surprisingly, there are two opinions among the most successful networking leaders. Some say, let the new distributor go. Let them act on their instincts and use their initial enthusiasm to sign up as many friends as they can. But the majority of leaders agree that it is much better to wait.

First, see how you do. And constantly check with your more experienced team partner. If what you are saying isn't working, then stop. Think it through. Talk it over with your team partner and try a different approach.

On the other hand, if what you are saying works well, also stop and bring it to your sponsor. You may be promising something that isn't true or won't happen.

Remember, make sure it is true. And if he or she says, yes, keep going, get back to work and keep setting up those meetings.

Step 11

If involving a married couple, invite both the husband and wife.

Today, some of the largest networks in the world have been built by women, on their own, without any help from a husband or male business partner. Some even argue that women are better networkers than men, that they are more adept at relationships, that men are often blinded by the apparent contradiction of numbers in building a networking business.

But today's network marketer should not forget a guiding principle that worked well in the early boom of this industry. When possible, invite both the husband and the wife to see and hear about your opportunity.

Here's the principle to keep in mind. If you show it to just the husband or the wife, even if they react favorably, the other partner will likely reject it when they hear about it. On the other hand, if you show it to both the husband and the wife, there is a slightly higher chance that one is likely to pick up on the idea and defend it. Thus you slightly increase the odds of success by sharing it to both.

Step 12

Get into a Network Marketing educational system.

It's pretty hard to build a Network Marketing business by yourself. As you will learn, the largest networks are built with powerful and effective educational systems. These are organizations that have books, CD's, training materials and inspiring speakers who can train and motivate your new recruits. If you are part of a good educational system, you can concentrate on recruiting friends and feeding them into the program.

This almost always involves CD's, books and regular meetings that take place monthly.

When you are building a business on your own, it is very dependent on your schedule, your attitude, your knowledge, your commitment. If you get your people plugged into a system, they can grow at their own pace. You may be gone for a few weeks and come home to find an even bigger network than you left behind because your leaders were plugged into a system that continued to teach them and help them grow as network builders.

A system can teach your people many things that you can't teach yourself. A speaker may talk about personal hygiene which would be confrontational coming from you directly. Or a speaker may talk about the importance of being loyal to your upline and to show respect to the person who recruited you into the network. You can hardly do that yourself. But a speaker at a systems event can do it effectively. And leaders with greater or different experience can teach principles and methods that you haven't yet learned. Why limit your network to your own experience?

We have found in networking that distributors tend to project on other people what they are going through themselves. And sometimes this works. If we don't have money we will say, "Our people can't afford that function," or "They can't afford that CD. Our people are broke."

Or we'll say, "Yes, our people can come to the convention in Paris" because we have money and can come ourselves. The problem is that everybody in your group is not the same. They are not all broke at the same time, they're not all hungry at the same time, they're not all anxious to build at the same time, they don't have their prospect list ready at the same time. There are different seasons.

Someday you may have a distributor who is ready to go, ready to build a great organization. But you can't help them because you're having a wedding. If they miss their opportunity, you miss your opportunity. Now, if you have them plugged into a system and they are going to functions and getting the materials, the steady diet of the CDs they need to build their business, then they'll grow even bigger while you're at the wedding. They will be at a function and come back with pages full of notes and ideas to do even more.

That's what you want. You don't want to be the boss of a business, you want to retire to the beach. The way you get to the beach is when people are growing at their own pace, at their own time, without being held back by what you're doing. They are not being limited by you. At any point, you can get back in and help them and you should do that often. But if you can get them into a good system it will take them further than you can by yourself.

Let's call the educational system a school. Somebody will be great at geography, somebody will be great at science, and somebody will take the language class. You'll be surprised at where their talents emerge.

But if you keep them locked in your basement, where you spoon feed them the information you choose, letting them out only occasionally, you'll eventually lose them. If you give them up to a system that will teach edification, teach loyalty, teach these principles of networking, someday that system you have promoted will give you back a ballroom full of people. And you will be making a lot of money.

Step 13

Read positive books.

A close friend of mine, Charlie Jones, once said, "Five years from now you will be the same person you are today except for the books you read and the people you meet."

Today, with the explosion of the Internet we have no excuses. Information is everywhere. And it is often free. But what we read and listen to will impact our lives and ultimately affect our decision making.

Here are a few Proverbs from the Bible. "You can look at a mirror but if you really want to know what you are like, look at the friends you choose."

Here is another. "He who walks with the wise, grows wise."

No one denies the power of our peers. Our friends will put us in prison or bring us to the palace. Our future and our destinies are linked to the people around us. But we do not have to be prisoners of chance. We can link to the greatest minds of the universe by reading what they have written. We can transcend our own circumstances by "walking with the wise."

Abraham Lincoln did just that. For fourteen years he lived in a log cabin in the woods of Indiana. He had to walk a mile each morning to get water for the day. For most of those years he slept in corn husks. The cabin had no floor and it had a bear skin as a door.

But Lincoln had five books. Aesop's Fables was one. The Bible was another. And so young Lincoln, whose father was abusive, knocking him to the ground with his fists, and whose stepmother was illiterate, "walked with the wise." He practically memorized those books.

Read positive books and you will become a positive person and your network will grow just as you personally grow.

Step 14

Practice showing the plan.

Just as you practice to invite someone to meet with your upline team partner, practice to show the plan yourself, both as one-on-one in conversation with friends and as a public presentation. Keep in mind the formula.

1.) It should be true. Don't misrepresent your plan. Remember, if you are in a legitimate company you will only make money when your prospect eventually makes money and then a small percent of their income. So why be dishonest or manipulative?

2.) It should be you. Show the plan in a way that is comfortable, that you believe, that does not violate your personality and who you are.

3.) It has to work. If no one gets in, stop. Go no further. Get advice from a networking leader in your company and find out what you can change to make your presentation more effective.

Some people hate to speak in public and will do anything to avoid it. In fact, it is often identified as the single greatest fear that most people have. And if you are a good organizer, doing all the work behind the scenes, you can avoid it.

I once spoke for a great Network Marketing leader. He had 90,000 of his distributors gathered at a great event in Indianapolis, Indiana. He was very shy and hated speaking publicly. And yet he had built one of the largest networks in the world.

Even so, practicing what you will say will be very useful and if you can overcome this fear you can speed up the process of your growing network.

Step 15

Get some friends to see you rehearse the showing of the plan.

If you are going to learn how to show your business opportunity then you eventually need to practice on a live audience. Explain to some of your friends that you are developing this business and your team partner is insisting you practice showing the plan before a live audience. As fearful or as uncomfortable as you may be, this is something you feel you have to do. Would they be willing to be your audience?

Of course, if you do a good job, they just may decide to join you in the enterprise. And don't hesitate to sign them up.

Step 16

Audit other presentations.

Once again, experience is the key to success in anything. And the more business plans you see and hear the better equipped you will be to make a presentation yourself. Ask your upline mentor - team partner if you can audit some other distributors showing the plan, just so you can see how they do it and what they say. You might as well learn from other's mistakes and successes in addition to your own.

Notice, you should not just show up unannounced to see someone else's presentation. If you are going to work with a team partner you need to trust them. And they will know who gives the best presentations and why.

Sometimes in a networking business there is predatory behavior. And there are different methods and systems that can confuse your group. When it comes to auditing another distributor's meeting, rely on your upline partner for guidance.

Step 17

Start a meeting in your own home.

Some Network Marketing companies encourage their leaders to set up offices and bring their prospects in for presentations. There are real advantages to this.

The office looks impressive. The presentation is taking place on your ground and you can create and control the environment.

Even so, most of the largest networks in the world have been built in people's homes and apartments.

The traditional method is to find someone who wants to launch a network and have them invite friends to their apartment or home. Then you or your upline mentor come in as the guest speaker and show the plan.

It works because many of the prospects will know where their friend's apartment or home is. In some cases they have already visited. They know how to get there, where to park if driving, how to get transportation if they need to. The process is more comfortable.

Step 18

Get the meeting out of your home.

Now, we are going to share an important concept that is elusive to most networkers. It could change your life as a businessman or woman so read carefully. You want to get a meeting in your own home but you also want to get that meeting out of your home. You don't want to get stuck in one place having meetings over and over with the same people in the same location. The key to building networks is to keep the process moving.

Let me explain. Suppose you start a meeting in your own home and it's a huge success. There are cars lined up down your block. The neighbors are so upset by the disruption that they call the police. Your room is so crowded that the room temperature is stifling hot. And people are excited. Many are joining your network and the word is spreading.

Eventually, after the months pass and the years pass, the home meeting will decline.

In five years the house meeting that was so dynamic now has a small gathering of ten people coming. The excitement is gone.

On the other hand, let's say you start it in your house and nobody comes and you have a no-show three weeks in a row. Finally some old lady comes and brings her bird. You're trying to convince her and her parrot to join. If you keep working with her and her friends, in five years you will eventually have a small group of ten people coming on a regular basis.

One started strong and the other started slow but both ended up about the same. So why go through all this work if you're only going to only end up with the same ten? If the groups go up and fall down how does anyone ever make any money?

And here's the answer. After a few weeks, get it out of your house and into the house of one of the person's coming to the meetings. And when you start a new meeting in their house, watch for someone else to help you start a new group in yet another house as well. If you keep opening new meeting places you will find that in five years there will be a hundred house meetings with ten distributors in each and you will find your network growing exponentially.

Some people get stuck in their meeting place. Maybe they have a beautiful home that shows like a mansion and gives great credibility to the business you are building. Maybe you have an office with a great location and easy access. Use it. Use the credibility and use the location. But if you become wedded to the location you will not build a dynamic network.

A network is an organic business that will grow its own unexpected way. It may involve people and places that you never expected. It may move to a city or a village that is new to you.

Now, this doesn't mean that your fine home or your perfect office location cannot be used again. Just start a new group there. But keep it moving, too. Follow it to other locations and other leaders as well.

Get the business in your home. But get it out into someone else's home as quickly as you can.

Step 19

Get a new face into your group.

No matter how talented you are or how much credibility you have or how entertaining and effective your presentation of the networking plan may be, it will be hard to do it alone. You need another face. Remember the Chinese proverb: If you want to go fast, go alone. If you want to go far, take someone with you.

People will quickly grow tired of your humor, less tolerant of your mistakes and faults, and they will grow bored with you and your personality. Even before you launch your group it is a good idea to sit down with your upline mentor or the person your upline mentor has assigned and approved to work with you and together plan out the first two months.

As you begin your groups you will be promoting the dream, networking plan, the company, the products, but second only to the dream you will be promoting the team or the people who will be working with you.

Tell your group how lucky you are to have such help. Remember how and why to promote this person. And if you do it right, when they come in to speak to your group, you will have a good attendance.

Sometimes an upline mentor will arrange for you to work with someone else in his group, a colleague crossline from you. If it is approved upline, where it can be monitored by someone who directly benefits from your success, then there is no problem. In fact, the perfect team is three. Each can help the other by coming in and providing some outside magic.

Remember, when you start a new group, regardless of the initial enthusiasm, the seeds of death are already there. The group will soon become bored. Have your team ready and bring in a new face.

Step 20

Make sure the new face is loyal to you.

Now, you don't want just any face. You want someone who understands this is your group, it represents your prospect list and the prospect of your people.

The primary purpose of this outsider's visit is to promote YOU and your people. In fact, that is the one thing you cannot do effectively yourself. He or she should be telling the group about you and why they are lucky to have you helping them build a network.

If the "new face" is not promoting you and your group, then no matter how effective they are at showing the plan, or how entertaining they are as a speaker, you need to have a private talk. You need to remind them of why they were invited in to talk to your group. If they don't understand then you are working with someone who is either attempting to steal your group or ignorant of how networks grow and in either case, you need to get someone else.

Step 21

Have someone else introduce you at the meeting.

Nobody can promote themselves. It will make your meeting more effective if you have an assistant, someone who arranges for everything and actually introduces you. This person is very important because they are setting the stage for what happens next.

Don't leave this role to chance. Again, try to find someone loyal, someone who understands networking enough to know why giving you credibility will help them and the whole group as well. If you can start off with an advantage, your presentation will be all the more effective.

If "the assistant" is older than you, better educated than you, more professional than you, it will work even better. The audience will see the respect that this person has for you and will be impressed. But for it to work "the assistant" has to humble him or herself and promote you.

Some networkers don't like presenting the opportunity themselves but they are good at promoting others. Use your gift, whatever it may be. Do what comes naturally. If you prefer to be "the assistant", play that role well.

Step 22

Develop your own signature.

Remember Step Number Nine? How it is important to learn how to promote you upline team partner? Well, it is important to find a short, easy, powerful way for you to be promoted as well. Every networker needs to have this "signature."

A friend of mine had been in networking for many years and had built many groups. One day he sat down and totaled up the volume he had generated as a network marketer. It was over $2 billion. And so we started calling him "the two billion dollar man." It was true and it was short and it was powerful. Who wouldn't want to hear what he had to say?

If you review Step Number Nine you will remember that you can promote anyone. And anyone can promote you. Perhaps you are just getting started and you have no credentials at all. You can be promoted as "one of the most knowledgeable new distributors in our network. She knows more about the business than many who have been working for years."

Or someone may say, "This man works closely with one of the most successful networkers in Southeast Asia. The networker is a millionaire and this man is one of his closest confidantes."

You might say, "This woman works harder than any I have ever known in years of Network Marketing. She will be a legend within a couple of years. If she agrees to take you on as a distributor you will be a success because no one outworks her."

Decide what you want to be. Michael Jackson was known as "the King of Pop." Why? Because he said he was. He started calling himself the King of Pop and had his public relations people do it, too. Imagine the nerve? And then other people started repeating it and soon it became accepted by the world. No one complains. No one gripes, what a smart aleck little brat he was to call himself the King of Pop. Because it was repeated over and over, it was enough.

Now, it worked because he came close to that very signature. But you too, with a little humility and a little imagination, can crown yourself. Just find the words that fit and make sure they are repeated.

Step 23

Listen to a positive CD before showing the plan.

How many times are you reminded, "Don't forget to eat!" The fact is you don't have to be reminded very often because you will know when you are hungry and you will do something about it.

But our attitudes will drag us down with little warning. They send out no hunger pains. But they also need to be fed or they will become negative and fill our minds with doubts and worry.

Before you show the plan? Eat something. In this case, take something for the soul. Listen to a positive CD before showing the plan and feed off of the energy and hope throughout the evening. This will increase the odds of your success and make your time all the more effective.

Step 24

Have your upline teach your downline what they need to know.

The shortest distance between you and your downline is through your upline. The fact is that your new recruits are not going to be very impressed with what you know about Network Marketing. No matter how wealthy and successful you may be, you are a novice to this industry and they know it. Better to play humble and promote your upline mentor and have him or her come in and teach the things that need to be taught.

Now that doesn't mean that you can't be pulling the strings behind the scenes. You can tell your upline mentor what is going on and what you think needs to be done. But be willing to be corrected. And when your mentor does say what needs to be said, don't be surprised when your distributors are amazed, acting as if it is the first time they ever heard it. That is the nature of network building.

Your kids will listen to anybody except you.

Step 25

Look successful.

Make a good impression by what you wear and how you look. A recent survey showed pictures of two businessmen to a focus group. One of the men clearly had the better success record and the most impressive resume. The other dressed better and looked better. Well, you probably have guessed what happened. The participants in the focus group were asked who they wanted to work with and they all picked the one who looked the best.

Make sure you dress as appropriately as possible and brush your teeth. Look good and you will have won half the battle.

Step 26

Learn how to do one-on-ones.

There is no reason why you should have to wait for others to build your network. Just as you learn to show the plan to a group, learn to show it one-on-one to an individual.

Try out your presentation on a friend. Each time you share it you will get better at anticipating the objections.

Make sure you begin by asking questions. And listen carefully. In many cases your prospect will say something that will be an opening for you and allow you to share the plan. Some of the most talented networkers are good listeners, not good talkers.

Step 27

Give a prospect a unique reason to get into your business.

Why should a prospect join your business? To make money? But what are the odds that they will be successful? If you say that you have a great company, with great products and you can prove it, that may only be intimidating. It may actually discourage a prospect who doesn't feel that he or she will make the commitment to make your business work.

Your business opportunity is an unknown for them. Why do they want to be in YOUR group, one of YOUR distributors? Why aren't they the upline? Sure it will work for you but will it work for them?

You say, "Our company has a million distributors." But your company's success does not guarantee the prospect's success. They may not want to be one of a million distributors, a little ant slaving away for the master, a laborer, toiling all day to build the Pyramids for some Pharaoh.

The solution is to offer each and every prospect a unique reason to get into your business. Something special that applies only to them.

When I built my first network I sponsored a chiropractor. He came to our meetings for one reason. He was looking for new patients and he thought by participating in a networking business he would make friends and when they needed him they would come calling. It worked. He built his chiropractic business but his network grew in the process. He eventually quit his profession and enjoyed the freedom he got from his networking business.

Perhaps the best reason for someone to join your network is your upline team. By promoting your upline mentor and the close team you have assembled to build a network, you are offering your prospect something that no one else coming into the same company will have. You can tell the story of how you connected and why this unique set of circumstances brought you together and why that portends success for the prospect.

It is one thing to come into a great company with a great opportunity. It is something else to stumble onto a team that is dynamic and knowledgeable and willing to help do the work. That is unique. It is an opportunity that no one should waste.

Step 28

Sponsor your weakness.

If you are shy and find you just can't talk to people, don't despair. Just sponsor your weakness, that is, sponsor someone who is outgoing and not afraid to talk. If you are disorganized and hate doing the paperwork that your company requires, don't despair. Just sponsor your weakness. Find someone who loves all of those details and can take the paperwork and make sense out of it.

I have a friend who built one of the world's most successful networks. He filled the largest auditorium in his country and filled it many times over. And he did it as a young man. By the time he was in his thirties he was living in a castle in France with a fleet of beautiful cars. According to his story, he started putting his network together while still a student in college. He didn't have his own car so he had to take a bus all over town.

"It must have been pretty tough," he was asked. "As your network started to grow across the country, and you just a student. And not even owning a car."

"Well," he said. "It was an easy problem to solve. I just made sure the people I sponsored owned cars."

Don't know how to promote people? Sponsor someone who does. Can't give a good presentation? Sponsor someone who can. Too young? Sponsor someone older. Too old? Sponsor someone younger. No education? Sponsor an academic. No good at sponsoring people? Well, sponsor someone who is.

Don't despair. You can solve almost any problem in networking by sponsoring someone new. And they don't have to be cookie cutter copies of you. Sponsor your weakness.

Step 29

Calibrate your prospecting approach.

Be ready to change your sponsoring approach based on the marketplace. If it is difficult to sponsor people and you have talked to your upline mentor and he or she agrees that it is a resistant marketplace, then you need to make it easier for a prospect to get into your business.

On the other hand, if you are overwhelmed with work and have phone calls coming in and distributors who need help, you can start to qualify your prospects to make sure that you have someone who won't waste your time and will do the work. Be careful. It is difficult to "qualify" someone. Many of the greatest leaders in networking would have been easily overlooked as ordinary.

So how do you make it easier for a prospect to get into your network? It's very simple, you promise them more help. In fact, if you promise enough help they would be foolish to turn you down. You are, in effect, working for them, planning their networking strategy, making calls, visiting with people, all to build them and their income. And they don't have to pay a salary. Who would turn that down?

Step 30

Sponsor peer and above.

This is one of the great principles of successful networking but it is sometimes difficult to do. As much as possible, you should sponsor people with your level of education, income and social standing or those who have even better education, income and reputation.

Why? Because when you sponsor people who you easily influence you are communicating that you don't really believe in your business for yourself but rather for others who are less successful. You are communicating that they will work for you and bring you in extra income, but if it really worked successfully, you would be sharing it with your friends and colleagues.

In my own network I had a very successful banker who drove a good automobile and lived in a beautiful home in the best neighborhood. He got in a networking business with me because he said he wanted to help his son get something going. He said if he had the same opportunity as a youth it would have changed his life today.

His network started off fairly well but then immediately died. He encouraged his son to sponsor people but never once shared his opportunity with colleagues or his own friends. Unintentionally, he gave the impression that "this business is great for young people but won't really work for me and my friends." He seemed above it all, too important. The business was for kids.

Another very successful lawyer in my group was a brilliant, classy, well dressed man with a great family. He was bright and affable and friendly but his network floundered. One day he asked me what he might be doing wrong.

Well, I ran down the litany of networking principles. Was he listening to CD's, going to functions, using the third party principles? And he said yes to all of those. He was genuinely perplexed.

But then I asked, "Well, are you sponsoring peer and above?"

He paused, and thought about it. "No," he said. "I'm not doing that."

As a lawyer he was assigned cases of young men in trouble and he had felt that networking was the perfect business for them. No employer would see that they had a criminal background or had made mistakes with their lives. It was a chance to start over with unlimited opportunity, regardless of their past.

Now, all of that was true. And he found it quite easy to sponsor these young men because they were dependent on him. But he was communicating to his peers that he really didn't believe in the network for himself. Otherwise he would be sharing it with them.

I shared this principle at an event in the United States and a young lady in the audience immediately identified with what I was saying. It was like a light switch coming on. "That's it," she said to herself, "That's what I am doing wrong."

Not long afterwards she was on a flight sitting next to a handsome young man, and as they talked she learned that he was a world champion athlete featured on the cover of magazines and a household name in Brazil.

"Well," she said, "You need to be associated with a Network Marketing company."

He talked to her about it and she realized that he thought she meant that he should get a bonus and big money for an endorsement.

"No, no," she said. "The money from endorsements is soon gone. You need to take advantage of your popularity and fame right now to build a network for yourself, a network that will give you a monthly income for the rest of your life."

Within three months she had sponsored some of the most famous athletes in Brazil.

Step 31

Teach all of the networking principles, not just the ones that work for you.

This is a good time to talk about what you should share with your group. Now, keep in mind, your own friends and personally sponsored distributors will not be impressed with you no matter how successful you become. You will need a "third party," someone else to come in and teach them. But your "grandchildren" in the network, that is the distributors who are brought in to your network in depth by others, may be ready to hear what you have to say. So what should you teach them?

The answer is that you should teach all of the networking principles, even the ones that you haven't mastered. Maybe you don't sponsor peer and above, that should not stop you from teaching its truth to your group. None of us are perfect as network builders, all of us have weaknesses. But don't assume that your weaknesses apply to everyone else and don't assume that your strengths can work for others, too. Each of us are different.

Teach all the principles of networking success and let the distributors in your group soar as high as they can go. Let them decide how big they want their network to be. Don't retard their growth by holding back information. Give them what they need to be successful.

Step 32

Learn to teach how to lead, rather than how to build.

There is an old proverb that says this: "People want to learn, but they don't want to be taught."

We have already discussed why and how to have a third party, an upline mentor for your group, someone to teach networking principles. Your own personal friends are not ready to accept you as an authority on Network Marketing. But when a third party isn't available you can still teach prospects and new, personally sponsored distributors by using an indirect approach. Instead of telling them what to do, treat them as a leader and share with them what they should teach their group.

The wrong way? "You should make a list of contacts."

The right way? "You will want to teach your new prospects to make a list of contacts."

You begin by treating your prospect as if they are already a leader and that they have a phantom network out there. You are telling them what they will want to teach their people. Thus the approach is indirect. They don't feel demeaned for you laying out the plan. And they may feel inspired to imagine their network growing. The most important thing is that they will see why they, too, should do these things as an example for the network yet unborn.

Step 33

Know when to take charge.

While the previous principle works well, especially when you are sponsoring peer and above, you must be willing to take leadership of your group when they are ready. And when you take charge you should teach the important networking principles openly and with confidence but without guile or becoming personally involved with individual cases.

There are a number of times and ways for you to take the lead.

1.) When you are not sponsoring peer and above but are sponsoring distributors who look to you for leadership and guidance. Don't hesitate, let them know what will work and why.

Remember it is better to sponsor peer and above and to use an upline mentor and a third party partner but if you have not done that, if you have sponsored people who look to you for leadership and direction, then you better lead the way and tell them what to do next.

2.) When your upline mentor tells you that you are ready and is encouraging you to take leadership and is promising to publicly support you in your new role.

3.) When you are becoming frustrated by the mistakes and wasted time as other distributors are building incorrectly.

4.) When you feel ready and want to take the lead.

Step 34

Follow up within the first 48 hours and never wait more than three days.

When you prospect someone, you must follow up within a day or two. Never wait more than three days. If you delay you are signaling that you are too busy to help them or to even care what they think about your idea.

Most of us delay in the follow up because we dread to hear what they will say. In many cases they have talked it over with friends and will come back discouraged or with fresh objections, or they will say they are too busy and have changed their mind.

If you are psychologically ready for this, if you go into the process knowing that this is normal, that alone will take away some of the pain and fear of the follow up. Don't be afraid of rejection. You are one person closer to an important link in your network.

Don't delay. And be prepared to listen closely to what they say.

If you do experience rejection, don't just ask them why they changed their mind. They may not tell you the real reason anyway. Rather, ask them what part of the idea they did like. Tell them that it will help you to understand your own business better. And the answer to that question may give you an opening for further discussion.

Step 35

Use your products.

You should never join a company that produces bad product. That is a given. But once you have made the decision that the products are effective, be loyal to them. Order them, use them. Never betray doubt to your downline about them.

If you use them you will find a way to talk about them. And if you talk about them, they will sell to friends and relatives and your growing network.

Step 36

Talk about your products.

Some distributors make the claim that they cannot sell. The fact is, we all sell all the time. We sell when we talk about something. We sell a book we read, a movie we saw, a restaurant we liked. We sell schools and teachers and learning methods for our children. We sell dentists and doctors and remedies and ideas. We sell apartments and homes and automobiles and public transportation. And yes, we sell product, cosmetics, clothes, computers, telephones, vitamins and detergents. When we talk, we are almost always selling. So learn to talk about your products and they will sell.

Step 37

Categorize your new distributors as business builders or product people.

When you signed up a new distributor, did they get in because of your business model, to build their own network and have a residual monthly income? Or did they sign up to get the products at a discount?

Depending on the company and your situation, you may want to develop two groups. One will follow networking principles and build their own business, and the other will concentrate on how the products work and why they work. They will tend to promote the sales of those products.

Now both groups will not work exclusively within their box. The network business groups will obviously promote product or there would be no income. And the product groups will also talk about the business model and how you can sponsor others. The difference is in the degree of emphasis.

The reason you want two groups is so that they won't confuse and demoralize each other.

There is nothing really wrong with the product group. They are like your customers. They make the whole business work.

But their activity is easier. It involved no risk of failure and rejection. It will be very seductive for your business builders to spend their time with friends talking about products. Your income depends on the business groups, distributors who will strive to build a network and who are seeking a larger, residual income that is not dependent on how much they sell that month.

Arrange separate meetings for the two groups and try to keep your business builders focused on networking.

Step 38

Revisit distributors in the business-product categories.

Sometimes a product person will reach a time in their life when they need more income. Don't forget to revisit your product people and remind them of the compensation plan. You can recruit new business builders right from your own ranks, from the product people in your network.

Likewise, some of your business builders may grow tired and discouraged by the process. They may even drop out. Involving them for a short time with the product may rejuvenate them and bring them back. But don't mix the two groups. Maintain the integrity of your system.

Step 39

Never let a prospect get away without a referral.

When you share with a new prospect, whether they say yes or no, make sure you ask for a referral. Do they know anyone else who might be interested in your business?

It accomplishes several things at once.

First, it gives you a second chance to talk about the plan as you explain why their friend might be interested and what it could mean to them. This time they are less threatened because they are not the focus of your discussion.

Second, it gives them a graceful way out. If it is confrontational and difficult for you to experience rejection from a prospect, it is also sometimes awkward for the prospect to say no. They just might offer you a referral as compensation.

Third, it keeps your prospect list alive and gives you yet another chance to sponsor someone else.

Of course, if they say yes to your plan, then the person they refer should be sponsored into their organization.

Now, all of this applies to product as well. If your prospect says yes or no to the products, ask for a referral from them as well. And all of the same reasons apply.

Step 40

Help your new distributor make a list.

If you sponsor someone who has lots of energy and belief in your business and someone who has lots of experience in networking, they may resent too much attention and direction from you. They may want some room to try things out. But most of your new recruits will be utterly dependent. And the smart networkers, the ones with experience, will want to hear your every suggestion.

So don't leave your growing network to chance. Just because you have sponsored someone doesn't mean that your job is finished. They have probably joined because they believe in your energy. They believe that you will do the work. Don't worry, you won't have to do it all forever. When their network gets going they will duplicate you and take the initiative. For now, stay with your prospect and help them in each of the steps we have been discussing.

Sit down with your new distributor and help them make a list of prospects. Have them talk about these people. The more they talk about them and the more they think about them, the easier it will be to find a way to prospect them. Bring your upline mentor into the discussion by telephone or email or even in a visit. Your new distributor needs an audience, someone who cares about their success and about their rejection, someone who shares the adventure and the risk. Don't leave this process to chance. Be part of it.

Step 41

Rehearse the invitation with your new distributor.

Ultimately, you want your new distributor to lead you to other prospects. And just as you have helped them make a list, don't leave them alone in the process of inviting their friends and relatives into your business.

Tell your new distributor that you want to practice with them. What will they say to the prospects on their list? Will they invite them to meet you? Will they invite them to their home or apartment?

And just what will they say?

Practice with them. Give your own version of what to say even if you stumble and are clumsy. That may only empower them to do it themselves. And if you come up with some good words and good ideas they can mimic you. Have them try and then you again. And if you have successfully involved your upline mentor, have him or her try as well.

There is no rejection in rehearsal. And remember, the success comes in practice. It is not the will to win but the will to prepare to win that leads to success. By practicing together you are building a relationship. When your new distributor picks up the telephone to call their prospect, they are not alone. They remember your time of rehearsal and they feel you with them.

Step 42

Remember, you are responsible for everything.

Ultimately, you are responsible for all of this to work.

"What?" you may ask, "Isn't my upline responsible for some of this?"

The answer is that if you want to earn tens of thousands of dollars a month from your own network then you have to start playing the part now and acting and deciding as a network leader would act.

You should have someone else promote you but if that isn't happening then you have to make it happen.

You should have help from your upline mentor in finding the right team members to work with but if that isn't happening you don't wait for them. You persist until they answer. And if you can't get them to answer, you go further upline until you find someone who will. And if you can't find anybody in your company who cares about it, then you better get another company.

Your upline leaders should be promoting the training CD's and functions but if they aren't doing that then you need to step up and do it yourself.

You have a choice, you can blame others for not doing their job and sit and pout or you can get it done yourself and train your team how you did it.

Don't wait. Don't let other people, upline or downline, decide your future or when you will be successful. Don't let them chose your lifestyle, the car you drive, the school your children attend, the home where you live. You make those decisions and you can make those decisions if you are successful. But your success depends on what you do, not what others do.

Don't be deceived into thinking that someone else will make you successful. You have to decide. You have to act. And you have to make all of these principles work for you. Anything that comes from others is extra.

Assume your responsibility as a leader. Don't shrink from it. You had to be a parent and maybe when that baby arrived you didn't know what to do. There were no written instructions. And maybe they didn't have Google back then. You just suddenly had a baby and you had to learn how to change its diaper. And you had to learn a lot of other things immediately. How did you do it? Why didn't anybody tell you what to do? Why wasn't there more teaching? Here you are, you're a mother, you're a father, but you had to assume responsibility for the sake of that baby.

When you sponsor someone in Network Marketing, you can't just throw it all upline. Of course we use a third party upline mentor, and we use "phantom upline" as you will learn later, but ultimately the responsibility is yours. You are responsible for everything that happens in your organization. You, alone, will earn the money. You, alone, have to do the work.

Step 43

Set long term and short term goals.

Building a network is easier when you know where you are headed. Thankfully, most Network Marketing compensation plans already have long term and short term goals set in place. But no matter how experienced and careful the corporate planners may be, each compensation plan works a little differently in the field than anticipated in the board room. It is the networking leaders in the field, the ones who have been able to make money, who can show you the way to maximizing your monetary return on your plan.

A wise networker will sit down with the upline mentor and learn everything he or she can about what the goal should be. It will help you streamline your time and investment. Why should you spend money and time learning the lessons that your upline mentor already has learned? And he or she has a vested interest in your success. If you succeed, they too will succeed. There is no reason for them to mislead you.

Step 44

Develop good work habits.

Keep in mind you are only ninety days away from success. Because success, especially in networking, is the result of habit. And it takes ninety days to establish a habit.

Don't think in terms of years for your success. Just maintain the pace for the next ninety days. If you can do that, and if you do the right things in those ninety days, you will have established the habits that will carry you on to success no matter how long it takes.

Most Network Marketing plans can show you some income within ninety days. And most will let you reach a sizeable income in three years. But it depends on doing things the right way, so that when they are duplicated by others far beyond your personal touch, they will still bring growth.

Step 45

Get into a good field-oriented educational system.

Almost all networking companies see the development of a field-oriented teaching and training system. This is when the distributors themselves, as opposed to the company, develop a training program to teach their own fellow distributors what works and what doesn't and how to build their businesses cost effectively.

Keep in mind, there are bad educational systems. And there are systems that started out honorably but have become corrupted. Money is almost always at the heart of the problem, but sometimes a system will break down because of egos and personality conflicts and even personal misconduct.

Sometimes, with little changes, the company finds a device to withhold the money paid out through its own compensation plan. And some companies have very poor compensation plans to begin with. In these cases, distributors will turn to the educational system itself with the sale of CD's, books and functions to earn a living.

The reaction from some distributors has been to shun all field-oriented educational systems. But the only growing networks have them. And you will have little chance of success without such help.

Sometimes breakaway groups will try to improve on system principles. I remember a large group in California. The leaders had broken away from a very tyrannical and egotistical personality and in their reaction they began to teach that no one person should be promoted but rather the educational system itself.

I had been invited in to speak. In the green room I asked for the names of the leaders so I could respectfully mention them from stage. "No, no," I was told. "We don't promote our leaders, we only promote the system."

I was astonished. Here was an audience of 15,000 people and I was told not to mention a single name. Needless to say, the group plodded on for a few more years and then fell apart.

The evidence for a good educational system can be found in the results. A good program will produce newly qualified leaders on a regular basis. If there is no growth or no new stories, you will have a pretty good idea that the educational system is a poor one.

The solution is to seek guidance from your own upline mentor. He or she will succeed or fail based on your performance, and if you don't grow, they won't make any money from the company compensation plan itself or the educational system, either.

Step 46

Think of CD's as your employees, put them to work.

CD's are the most powerful tool you can use to speed up the growth of your network. Think of them as your own work force. They will prospect, recruit and sell products if you can keep them busy by loaning them out. Most importantly, they will help train and inspire leadership inside your network.

Of course, all of this depends on what's recorded on the CD. But if you are plugged into a positive, effective educational system, the CD's they provide will have powerful stories of success that give the secrets to fast growth.

A CD is less threatening than a personal meeting. The prospect is in control. They can listen to the CD at their leisure. They can stop it when they like. They can reject listing to it in the first place. It is all their choice. But if they do listen, they can't cross examine it. They will have to hear what it says.

Some feel that CD's are too expensive, but I have found them to be a bargain. Imagine having to pay someone to do the same work and you get the idea. And if you teach this principle to your group, at any given moment you can have CD's working for you all over the world building your network even bigger.

Step 47

Build a CD library.

As you collect more and more CD's with more stories of successful networkers, you will find that you have a useful archive for building your business.

You will have not just one prospecting CD but several. You will have a CD for a flight attendant, a plumber, a doctor. You will have one for a Catholic, for a Muslim, for a born-again Christian. You will have one for an intellectual and one for someone who eschews education. You will have CD's where the speaker has a different accent or even speaks a different language. You will be able to match the CD with the prospect.

Likewise, almost any problem in your group can be solved with a CD from your collection. If your group is not moving products, you will have a CD that inspires product use. If your group doesn't know how to work as a team, if they haven't learned the third party approach, you will have a CD that will explain how it works and why it is to their benefit.

If your CD's are like your employers, then your library of CD's will show that you have specialists, some gifted for a specific task.

This will allow you to teach hundreds and even thousands instead of one-on-one. And it will speed up the growth of your network.

Step 48

Lead by example.

As you continue your networking journey, you may find yourself more as the executive of a large company instead of running a mom-and-pop small business. This, because your network will be growing.

But keep in mind that what you do on a small scale with the persons around you is still critical to your larger business because it duplicates.

Some of the greatest networking leaders are still sponsoring long after they have built a secure, gigantic business because they have learned that it duplicates down through their organization.

Don't feel sorry for them. Don't conclude that they are working their life away. One of my friends flies first class all over the world staying in the world's greatest hotels, eating the world's best cuisine, traveling and meeting with his friends but sponsoring new people along the way. He is living out his dream and building his network at the same time.

Step 49

Go to the functions.

The building place for leaders is the functions. That is, the special events in a hotel ballroom or a coliseum or soccer stadium where distributors from all over come to share their experiences. Sometimes the corporation itself will have useful functions, but usually the best information will come at events where fellow distributors, working just like you, will be able to share their advice.

The marketplace is constantly changing and the methods for growth have to accommodate the changes.

Several years ago, my wife and I were invited to speak at a major event in Europe. The host was one of the greatest networkers in the world. I told my wife to watch carefully and see what he was doing, how he built his organization and what we could apply to our own business.

We arrived a week or so earlier and spent the time visiting, shopping and eating at great restaurants with our host. His bodyguards hovered nearby and there were business assistants running errands. So while we would sit outside at a lovely café, eating a leisurely meal, he would be working as well.

And what was his work? It was troubleshooting his big event. Keep in mind, all the people at the event were in his downline. There were thousands and thousands of people. But he wasn't talking about lighting and audio visual, or seating, or union fees at the venue, or parking, or the program. He was talking about how to get his new personally sponsored people to his event. He was building a new group and he knew how important it was for them to be at a training session like this. He knew that their lives could be changed. His work was sometimes arranging a new babysitter for someone who was cancelling at the last minute. Or it was working with an embassy to get the needed visa for the trip.

This really is the work of a great leader. Getting people to your event. If they come, you have increased the odds that they will develop the desire to build a network of their own and learn how to do it. You can spend three months of training and teaching and prodding, or you can just get them into a weekend of training and accomplish it all at once and far more effectively.

Step 50

Promote the functions.

Remember, everything is your responsibility. You can't just sit by and say, "My distributors won't go to the functions." It is up to you to promote them. And the best way to promote them is to promote the speakers and leaders who will be there. Try to get good CD's of the speaker for the upcoming event and promote them to your group.

You may feel that it's a lot of work trying to get your distributor to the function. And it may be a great expense for them. But if they go they will have sped up the process of growing their network by months. In the long run, it may be less expensive for both of you.

Statistics from many different companies all show that most networking growth takes place within ninety days of a major function. Don't fight the odds, have them working for you.

Step 51

Take your distributors with you to the function.

One of the best ways to make sure your distributors go to the function is to go with them. Make the trip a time of friendship. Find unique reasons for them to make the trip. Will there be tourist sight-seeing opportunities? Will there be shopping? Will the group plan on seeing a movie together?

Remember, everything is your responsibility. It is up to you to promote the functions and create a fun experience built around the event.

Step 52

Understand the dangers of crosslining.

When you attend functions, you and your group will meet distributors from other lines of sponsorship. Sometimes they will even be part of other "networking systems," groups that have their own recruiting methods and product sales ideas and even CD's. If they really understand networking and respect the principles of networking, they will be respectful of you and your group. They will be friendly and courteous but they will not promote or even talk about their methods and ideas for recruiting and building their networks. They will have learned well this cardinal rule of successful networking: "Never crossline."

There are several reasons why. For one thing, you can usually trust your own upline mentor since his or her success and income depend on your success as well. Their advice and counsel is most important. Now, there are exceptions. There are people who don't even act in their own best interest.

There are times when ego, emotion and passion transcend common sense. People can be self destructive. There are mothers who murder their own children. And there are upline mentors who can act selfishly and ignorantly. But generally speaking, you are foolish to ignore the counsel of your own upline mentor, especially when they want you and need you to be successful.

Second, the advice you get from someone new is not likely to be as sound as someone who knows you well and knows your group and your past experience. It can even be harmful.

On vacation, I became ill and visited a doctor who discovered that I had high blood pressure. Now why hadn't my family doctor noticed that? Was this something new? I was impressed and grateful to my "vacation doctor". But when I presented my new medication to my old family doctor, he frowned. "Read your instructions," he said, and then passed the bottle back to me. I had other health issues as well and as I could now read for myself, my new medication was going to complicate things greatly. My "vacation doctor" had been right about the high blood pressure but didn't know enough of my medical history to find the right solution. Anything new, no matter how good it sounds, should be passed by your upline mentor, who is your partner, your advisor, as you build your network.

Third, sometimes even good ideas can destroy your network and nullify your work. Any change in method should be carefully studied and discussed with your upline mentor.

At the end of World War Two, American soldiers were horrified by the scenes they encountered in German concentration camps. The inmates who had been lucky enough to survive were skeletal and weak. The camps had been abandoned and there was no food available. The distraught soldiers gave inmates their own best rations, including salted bacon and beans. But the concentration camp inmates, who had been living on a potato diet, could not digest the rich food. They became sick and thousands of them died even as they had been liberated.

What will fatten one can kill another.

And finally, there are predators in Network Marketing who make their money by selling materials to crossline groups. Their own groups have died out and the only market left is others. They may not be good networkers but they are good writers, speakers and idea people. And they know how to sell their systems, CD's, books and training seminars. Some will charge thousands of dollars to "counsel" your people. This is not only a waste of good money, it can be very harmful to your growth.

Keep in mind there are exceptions to all of this. When your upline mentor arranges for outside speakers, he or she is only employing the same methods you use to build your own network. He or she is getting in a new face to teach principles that work. But at the same time, they are in control. They are helping to establish what will be taught and what materials will be sold, and they are able to protect you and your networks from exploitation. If their guest violates that trust, he or she will not be invited back.

Likewise, when your upline mentor encourages you to work with a distributor in another line, it is not crosslining because it is approved and monitored by someone higher up who has both of your interests at heart. Just as you will help the distributors in your network do things together to save money and time and to work more effectively. But unmonitored, self-initiated contact with crossline distributors can lead to disaster and is unanimously rebuked by the world's most successful network marketers.

Step 53

Pass negative upline. Pass positive downline.

When there are misunderstandings about the company or the products, or the upline organization or the educational system you are using, don't panic. The rule is to find out what's wrong and fix it. If the issues are intractable, if there is dishonesty or embezzlement or fraud, then make plans to get out of the company or break away from the networking system. In the meantime, don't pour your doubts or fears or speculation to your recruited downline. If you find that your suspicions are wrong, it will be too late to come back to them and repair the damage. It will be like trying to get salt back into a salt shaker.

Mark Twain once said, "Tell me what you believe. Keep your doubts to yourself."

The business of building a network is very rewarding but it is not easy. To be effective, a distributor has to have a good attitude and believe in his team and his company. You can fuel that process by being steady, positive, always believing in your distributor's success and protecting them from negative issues that need resolution.

By the same token, don't be gullible or in denial about any problems you see. Take them upline. And if the problems involved your upline, take them further and higher upline until you can find someone who will listen and try to resolve the issues.

Some leaders believe that it is just as important to pass negative upline as it is to pass positive downline. Why should you work in doubt if there are answers and explanations that will free you to work with enthusiasm?

One last thing, a very successful network leader recently told me that it is important to pass positive upline, too. If something is working, and if something is helpful, it is important for the upline to know. Your upline mentor is an emotional creature just as you are. And a little positive may help inspire them to work even harder.

Step 54

When you have no upline mentor, create one yourself.

Don't forget, you are responsible for all of this. You cannot blame your upline or your downline or your circumstances. If you want to have a great network with a bountiful income, you have to assume responsibility and start acting like a networking leader. You have to earn your money. But what do you do when you have no active upline mentor?

Perhaps you were recruited by a passing stranger in an airport and you are now isolated by geography, miles from any upline help or educational system.

Perhaps you have moved to a new city or village or a new neighborhood in a large metropolitan area and there is no one to help nearby. Perhaps the only upline mentor available has no time. You may be in a "leg" that is secure for them and it makes more sense for them to work in a weaker "leg."

Perhaps your upline mentor has had all the success they want and they are never available, always on vacation, or have retired altogether or even died. What do you do when there is no educational system, no functions nearby? How can you use these principles when you are by yourself? The answer is what I call "the phantom upline." You can still promote a third party, you can still show that you are submitted and being tutored by someone else, and you can still give your prospects and distributors a unique reason to join you and your team.

Now, I am certainly not advocating deception. There must be someone upline who will assume this role. But you are going to do almost all of the work. Explain to the "phantom upline" that you will write the emails. You will tell them what they need to say on any conference call. And you will keep their involvement to a minimum. Their main job will be to show up in person a couple times a year, do a few conference calls in between, and most important of all, promote you and speed up the transfer of leadership to you. In return you will give them a share of the income from any educational materials your network uses.

If your group sees that you are accountable to someone else, if they feel that they are connected to successful leaders, they will work with confidence.

Step 55

Remember, people will work for recognition or money.

While building your own business you will soon come to a new understanding of wealth. It is not necessarily money. Wealth is having what others want. It is having what is in demand. First food, but then weapons and tools, and eventually luxuries.

In England in the Middle Ages, wealth was wood. The forests were usually owned by the king or the nobility and wood was scarce for the commoner. At one time, furniture was so rare that it was hauled for the King from one castle to another depending on his residence. A person in England could be hung for stealing from a neighbor's woodpile. In the American West, wealth was your horse. A person would be hung for stealing a man's horse.

Most wealth is natural. It is coal or oil or gold or tin. Many areas of the world were colonized and natives put to work to extract the wealth from nature and bring it back to the mother country.

Men can also create wealth. When you create something that's in demand it becomes wealth. When man took tin and copper and mixed it and made bronze it was a huge leap in civilization. Bronze was softer and could be molded into ferocious weapons that gave an army an advantage. It was used to develop exquisite tools that could create jewelry and could do things that couldn't be done before. Likewise, man can create a computer from copper and plastic derived from oil.

One important way to capitalize your networking business is to create something that people want, recognition.

Soldiers in armies all over the world will work with great commitment for little pay and even risk their lives to move up to a higher rank or to be awarded medals and small pieces of colored cloth. Workers will labor for years to earn a new title or to get a better perk, maybe a better parking place or office. Youths will play computer games for days and weeks just to earn a higher rank that only they and a small circle of others can appreciate.

Now, it is against the law to print money. You can't just buy a laser jet printer and photo copy currency and start spending it. They will put you in prison. But there is no law against printing recognitions. There is no law against saying and doing and writing things that will honor other people. And remember, if your recognition is imaginative and sincere, they will work hard for it.

You may not have any money but you can capitalize your networking business to the tune of thousands of dollars by using this simple principle.

Promote your leaders when they reach the next level. Give them preferential seating at functions, honor them from stage, mention their name often. It will motivate others to work.

The most significant recognition is the recognition of peers. The young computer gamer wants the praise of his fellow gamers. A doctor wants the praise of other doctors. Julius Caesar often recruited soldiers from the same village because he knew that in the heat of battle they would not risk their lives for him and for a cause or for a nation, but they would risk their lives for their buddies who fought next to them.

As new prospects become immersed in the culture of your growing network, as they make friends, they will stay motivated and keep working if they know that someone is watching, that someone is keeping track.

Picture the little boy on the diving board yelling at his father who is relaxing nearby in the sun. "Hey dad, watch, watch. Dad? Dad? Watch, watch."

And when the father finally heeds his son's cry, he turns to watch as his son splashes into the water.

We all need an audience. And you are the father or mother to this growing brood of networkers. Your smile, your words of encouragement are like creating money out of the thin air. People will work to have them.

Step 56

Promote your system.

If you have successfully plugged into a networking educational system, or you have helped organize your own, then you need to learn how to promote it to your distributors.

Remember, all of the principles you used to recruit a prospect into your company and network now apply for this promotion as well. For example, you gave your prospects a unique reason to get into the company, some special connection that made them feel more important than an ordinary person. They were special, not just one of millions. Now, do the same in promoting your system. Share with them your inside connections and have your upline mentor do the same, explaining to the new recruit how lucky they are to have special help. If you take them to a function introduce them to the speaker. Have a party in your room after the event and have your upline mentor and maybe the guest speaker stop by to say hello.

Remember the formula we previously discussed. Your promotion should be honest and accurate, it should be natural and fit your personality and it should work, that is, it should produce results. If it isn't honest it will backfire and everything you do will come into question. If the promotion isn't natural, if it isn't you, then it will be hard to sustain. It will be like a new pair of shoes that doesn't fit. You will stop wearing them. And finally, you must find a formula that gets the desired result. Are they getting into the system? Do they use the CD's? Do they come to the functions?

Step 57

Help your downline set networking goals.

This may seem like an obvious principle but many distributors fail to do it. Perhaps it feels intrusive. They want to show respect to their distributors and not nag them. The best way to use this principle is with another leader. Bring in your upline mentor or a guest speaker whom your upline mentor approves or chooses. This may be an occasion to go to a leader further upline, one who is respected. Have them sit down with your distributors one by one, alone with only you and the mentor and the distributor in the room and talk about the future of their business.

If you have properly edified and promoted your upline mentor you will find that your distributor is more likely to open up. You will soon learn that he or she hasn't been telling you everything. What may surprise you is that there are other issues usually outside of the business, financial issues, relationship problems, children, health, marriage that have all been factors in their business performance.

It is important for you and the upline mentor to ask questions and then listen. Don't be quick to talk or take the lead. The more you listen, the more you will know about how to help motivate and teach your distributor.

This not only applies to their private, personal life, which is not yours to control anyway, but it also applies to networking where your expertise may lie. There will be the temptation to rush ahead and tell them what they should do and what their next goal should be and why. But first ask questions. You may be surprised by their answers. Ask them what their plans are. They may have more ambitious plans for themselves than you have. Let them talk. And if their goals are too timid, then afterwards, you can speak up and offer suggestions and give them more ambitious goals.

This whole process can be very powerful. For when everyone begins working at the same time, there will be group momentum and belief and new energy for the whole group. When each distributor takes small steps to meet their specific goals, the whole network begins to take giant steps forward and you begin to make money.

Step 58

Teach your downline how to promote.

We are back to this ongoing process of duplication. This is the key to successful networking. You simply cannot do everything yourself. You must duplicate, in fact you WILL duplicate. If you try to do it all yourself, your people will do the same and your group will soon be overwhelmed. If you learn to delegate responsibility and teach others how to do the work, they will likewise learn how to delegate and become teachers. Even so, remember, it is all your responsibility and the work has to get done somehow, so learn to delegate or be destined to do it all yourself.

Never forget why you are doing what you are doing and never fail to explain it and repeat it downline. You want them to promote the upline for their sake, not for the upline's sake, so it will help them create a sense of teamwork and uniqueness and so the new distributor will not feel alone. You want to promote the function so that their people will learn and become inspired to build their network even bigger. You want them to promote CD's because experience has shown that the groups who move the most CD's grow the fastest. Everything is for them, in their self interest. It is not for you and your upline and your system. It is for them.

And don't forget the principle of "teaching through them" to their group. Thus you are not lecturing them on what to do or reminding them of their new status but rather you are telling them that this is something they will want to teach their people. You are envisioning their network as it will become.

Once more, positive affirmation will have a big impact. Give recognition to the one who has the most distributors coming to an event. If they understand the business and are loyal to their line of sponsorship, they should get the speaking opportunities if they want them. They should get preferential seating on a bus trip to a function. They should be introduced and their work lauded. People will work for money and for recognition.

Step 59

Teach others how to promote you.

This is can be a very difficult thing to do. The people who find it easy usually get it wrong and come off as too egotistical. And the people who find it difficult usually mess it up as well, either not getting others to promote them enough or not promoting the right things.

It is hard to be objective about oneself. Some will just ignore this process altogether or leave it to chance. But remember, this is not personal. This is a business, albeit a networking business, and that involves people and people have egos. If you fail to get this right, you will pay the price.

In an earlier step we talked about developing a signature, a short one sentence way to promote yourself. But it won't work unless your own networkers pick it up and start using it.

All credibility is useful. If you hail from a great profession or have a good education or come from a prestigious family, it can all be used to promote you. And so can the opposite. For example, one of the most successful writer-teachers in the world tells about how he started out as a janitor. In a reverse logic it gives him great credibility. If a janitor can become a millionaire then maybe he knows something and I should listen.

In the same way your people can say, "Our upline came from a poor family and had no education but look at the success he is creating in Network Marketing."

Ultimately, it is your success in Network Marketing that should be the selling point. You may be the best doctor in the city. You may be a famous athlete. But your prospects are not in this business for you, they are in for themselves. And they want to know your credentials for building a Network Marketing business to see if you can really help them.

Once again, it is easier and more effective to have the upline mentor do this teaching. He or she should be the one to set your people down and teach them why and how to promote you and what words to use. But it is up to you to make sure this happens. Don't wait for your upline mentor to discover that this needs to be done. Tell them and make sure they do it.

Step 60

It's not what your upline does for you that will make you rich, but rather, what you do for your upline.

You may eventually have dozens of front line leaders and hundreds, even thousands, of distributors in your network. How you treat your upline mentor is how they will treat you. If you act like you are loyal but never let them know how cynically you really are about their leadership, they will act like they are loyal to you, without ever letting you know how cynical they really are about your leadership. You cannot stop the process of duplications.

I once spoke to a small group of networking leaders in Sydney, Australia. There must have been fifteen people in the room. They were hungry for information about the great leaders of networking and what they did and how they had become successful. At one point it descended into gossip. Who of these fabled leaders was really the wealthiest? I played along good naturedly sensing their feeling of isolation and feeling that the conversation was doing them some good. So I answered their questions and in the process learned something myself.

In case after case when there were two famous networkers, one the upline mentor and the other the downline leader, it was the downline leader who was actually the wealthiest. People in the audience didn't know because the downline kept pouring on the edification of the upline. I knew because I was a regular speaker for them both and a ghostwriter who wrote their books. One by one, they shot out a name of a great networking leader and it was matched with a downline who was even more successful.

And in each case, the downline had a reputation for loyalty. In some cases the reputation was undeserved. There were lawsuits and great animosity but nevertheless, this image of loyalty had to be part of their success.

I have spoken for groups that had 100,000 attending a great event and the upline leader bringing the event together had only 10,000 attending from his own network. The other 90,000 belonged to one of his loyal downline who was smart enough to bring him in and honor him as the leader.

A few years later, Mitch Sala, a great Australian networking leader, invited me back to speak to a coliseum full of his people in Sydney. We were in a leadership meeting when he passed me a note reminding me of that night of discussion long ago. He said that before the night was over he decided that he was going to be the most loyal distributor his upline ever had. It worked.

Step 61

Understanding the importance of momentum.

Occasionally, not very often but occasionally, you will experience fast growth. It can be compared to building a fire, although a fire is destructive and dangerous and what we are talking about is constructive and profitable. You start a fire with some twigs and then throw on some larger pieces of wood.

You can't expect a log to blaze until you get the twigs going. And when a fire does begin to grow you need more than one log to keep it going. Likewise, a network needs to experience these small beginnings and needs more than one good group to keep it company.

Never stop momentum. If a group is in the process of growing fast, never say to yourself, "Well, that group is secure, I will move on to the next." Momentum is a precious commodity and if you have it keep it going as long as you can no matter how big your particular networking group has become.

A time of testing will come to your network and the numbers will fall away faster than they originally came. If you have a large network group that is very deep with leaders whose incomes depend on its success, you will likely survive any setback and be in position to grow stronger again at the next surge.

Step 62

Keep in mind that it is hard to build more than three separate groups at the same time.

As your network starts growing, if you teach the right principles, you will eventually be in great demand. You will become the upline mentor we keep talking about in these pages. And you will be needed to give credibility and teaching to your downline. Just as children seldom take advice from their parents, your downline leaders will not usually be impressed by you. It will be left to you to teach the grandchildren, the distributors recruited in depth by your leaders. They will often want your help and advice and sometimes that is where you can be most effective.

The problem is numbers. While you may have five children, you could find yourself with eighteen grandchildren and no time to teach and mentor them all. Even if your compensation plan is a binary, you need to keep this principle in mind. Most leaders believe that it is difficult to build more than three separate autonomous groups or organizations at one time.

But as you will see, this does not mean that you should only sponsor three distributors.

Step 63

Sponsor fifteen to twenty to find your three.

Usually, to develop three strong groups you need to personally recruit fifteen to twenty new distributors. Don't panic if the first few don't grow at the pace you want. Not only are they learning but you are learning as well. And sometimes it has nothing to do with them or you, but rather circumstances in their life.

Some networkers, like parents, will devote all of their time to their firstborn child, or in this case, their first sponsored distributor. But a newer prospect sponsored into their business will take off with even less attention.

Be patient with this process. Keep sponsoring. Very seldom will your first three distributors be the three who will build the largest groups.

Step 64

Don't decide on leaders too quickly.

So if it is difficult to build more than three large groups at the same time, and you must usually sponsor 15-20 to find your three, then when do you make the decision? How big do your three groups need to grow for you to focus on them exclusively?

Many leaders differ on this subject. Some say you should never stop building all of your groups simultaneously, no matter how many you have. If you are overwhelmed, well, it is survival of the fittest. Those who survive will do so even without your help.

Most leaders will tell you to delay making the decision on which groups to build until the decision is forced on you. Above all, don't decide too quickly. Don't say, "These are my three groups." Wait as long as possible to decide.

A good doctor will delay in making his diagnosis because he or she has learned that once a diagnosis is fixed in their mind, all symptoms point to that diagnosis and seem to confirm it.

A good police detective will suspend judgment on a crime as long as possible. He or she will gather as much evidence and as many facts as possible before deciding what happened. The good detective has learned that once an accusation is made, all the evidence seems to confirm it.

Likewise, a good network leader will not jump to conclusions about which groups are the ones that deserve the most attention. A good networker will keep them all going as long as possible and will only begin to focus on the three largest groups when they themselves have forced their way to the top. And most networking leaders would add this thought: It is almost always a surprise.

Step 65

Get help in launching an out of town group.

It is very easy for a network to spread to other cities and communities. And then you are faced with the expense of building a group from far away. Some prospects will purposely send you to their relative or friend in some distant place so they won't have to work the network themselves. They may conclude, "Who knows, maybe it will work without me?"

You should keep the following in mind: While some out of town groups can grow on their own without much cultivation, just as some seeds can be thrown on the ground and germinate on their own, most groups need personal attention. It is wasteful to just throw seed onto hard ground and let the wind blow it where it wills. Likewise, it is a waste of time and money to sponsor someone in a distant city if you don't make the commitment to work with them to help them get started.

You need help in launching an out of town group. Talk with your upline mentor and get good advice before you make the commitment. While it is usually bad business to prejudge a prospect, and some of the most unlikely of them will surprise you and succeed anyway, you should only launch an out of town group with someone who looks and acts like a leader.

Step 66

Make your prospect build locally before launching an out of town group.

Don't just run off to another city for your prospect. You will soon go broke. Each prospect will pass you onto the next person in the next city so they won't have to do any of the work locally or carry any of the weekly responsibility.

Instead, tell your prospect that you will help him or her start an out of town group if they will do something local first. You will help plan the growth of the new city, arrange for its speakers, invest your time and money but you want the prospect to build a network locally so he or she will have experience and credibility to be the leader of this distant organization.

This "qualification" can be calibrated or changed depending on your time, money and availability. For example, you may be anxious to build in the city anyway, so you may waive any local requirement and just have all of your prospects put their names on your list. Or you can say, "Sign up five locally and we will help you launch another city."

People are more inclined to take responsibility and "ownership" if they have their own investment involved.

Step 67

Plan on making four weekly trips to launch an out of town group.

When launching an out of town group you should plan on making four weekly trips to get it started. Sometimes it will take more, sometimes it will take less. It depends on how hard you work when you are there and it depends on the desire and motivation of your local leader.

Now you, yourself, do not need to make all of these trips. In fact, as we have pointed out earlier, you need someone else to help you do this effectively. Your distant group will get bored with you and will wither and die. From time to time you need to have someone else go in your place. And remember, they should be loyal to you and they should promote you.

How can you do this?

By seeking help from your upline mentor. If your upline mentor can't do it, then go further upline to someone who can help. There is someone up there just like you, wanting to grow and here you come with your idea and your commitment to start a new city. It will help you but it will help them, too.

Your upline leader may have you do some meetings for them or another distributor nearby your own hometown. In return, they will get someone trustworthy from their bigger network to help launch your own out of town group.

Step 68

Plan on making a monthly trip for one year.

When launching an out of town group you should not only plan on making four weekly trips but you should plan on making a monthly trip for a year.

I know this sounds like a lot of trouble but actually, in the long run, an out of town group is less maintenance and less work than one nearby. The greatest networkers soon have large organizations in distant cities or even distant countries and continents.

One of the reasons an out of town group can be low maintenance is because of the nature of duplication. If you work hard, your group will work hard, too. An out of town group will duplicate what they see when you are with them. If you arrive in town for a day and work very hard while you are there, they will tend to do the same while you are gone. But if a group at home catches you taking a day off, they will soon be taking their own days off as well.

Even your monthly appearances should be interspersed with other speakers. Once again, you can find an upline leader to help arbitrate. You can speak for another leader nearby and he or she can speak for one of your out of town groups as well.

Eventually, as the group grows larger, they should pay for a hotel room and your travel expenses to the city. And within time, they should have enough income to pay you a fee for the visit. This is appropriate and fair.

Step 69

Visit your large groups at least once a year.

When an out of town group gets really large and has plenty of its own networking celebrities and its own network of speakers, you still need to visit once a year to retain your position as founder and to help arbitrate and solve differences. While your corporate contract may be inviolate, your leadership of a group depends on your reputation and your own relationship with its leaders. No one can make your group loyal to you. No one can force it to follow your teaching. If your work is not resonating with your out of town group, they may begin to look elsewhere for their leadership.

Step 70

Back up a distributor with a distributor.

Let's go back to basics and follow this principle all the way to the top of a large network of tens of thousands.

Always back up a distributor with a distributor. As soon as you sponsor someone new into your business you must focus on how to help him or her sponsor someone for themselves. You don't count on one distributor, you back them up with another. They are less likely to drop out because they have fear of loss. What if their own newly sponsored distributor does well?

Step 71

Back up a leader with a leader.

Now let's take this principle further. When you develop a leader, someone who has their own dreams and ambition and is savvy enough to listen to advice and learn how to build a network, don't stop with them. Help them develop a leader in their own downline. Someone who can help them build the network even bigger. Don't count on just one leader. Get another to back them up.

The same principle, the fear of loss, will apply. And two leaders will not do just twice as much as one, but rather the two leaders will do ten times as much as one.

Step 72

Back up a city with a city.

Now let's take this principle even a step further. Not only do you want to back up a distributor with a distributor, and a leader with a leader, but you also want to back up a city with a city.

Earlier in this book we talked about the dynamics of starting business opportunity meetings in your home or apartment. And I emphasized that the key to building a network was to keep it moving. Yes, you want to get a meeting in your own home but you also want to get that meeting out of your home. You don't want to get stuck in one place having meetings over and over with the same people in the same location.

I talked about how on some rare occasions you have a very successful start. Many show up for your meeting. There are cars lined up down your block. The neighbors are so upset by the disruption that they call the police. Your room is so crowded that the room temperature is stifling hot.

And people are excited. Many are joining your network and the word is spreading.

But as I pointed out, eventually, after the months pass and the years pass, the home meeting will decline. In five years the house meeting that was so dynamic now has a small gathering of ten people coming. The excitement is gone.

And the reverse is true. Let's say that you start your networking business in your house and nobody comes and you have a no-show three weeks in a row. Then that old lady comes and brings her bird. You're trying to convince her and her bird to join. If you keep working with her and her friends, in five years you will eventually have a small group of ten people coming on a regular basis.

One started strong and the other started slow but both ended up about the same. So why go through all this work if you're only going to end up with the same ten? If the groups go up and fall down, how does anyone ever make any money?

And the answer is this. After a few weeks, get it out of your house and into the house of one of the persons coming to the meetings. And when you start a new meeting in their house, watch for someone else to help you start a new group in yet another house as well. If you keep opening new meeting places you will find that in five years there will be a hundred house meetings with ten distributors in each and you will find your network growing exponentially.

The same process applies to city wide meetings.

After several months or even years of house meetings, you may finally be invited to join your groups with others and launch a citywide – monthly - opportunity meeting.

Remember, your meeting should be sanctioned and protected by an upline mentor who has negotiated your participation. You may want to re-read the principle about "Never crossline."

At first there will be great excitement. People will be thrilled to hear new speakers from other groups. There will be enthusiasm and excitement. But after a few years the meetings will begin to get boring and they will eventually die.

After five years, a great citywide meeting that drew thousands is reduced to a hundred. And a small citywide meeting that started with twenty is finally running a hundred as well. So what's the difference? All of that work and they end up in the same place.

The answer is to start a citywide meeting in another city.

Don't get stuck in one house or apartment. And don't get stuck in one hotel ballroom or office building. Maybe your meeting place is perfect in location and convenience. Use it. But don't become wedded to the location or you will not build a dynamic network.

A network is an organic business that will grow its own unexpected way. It may involve people and places that you never expected. It may move to a city or a village that is new to you.

Get the business into your city. But get it into someone else's city as well. Back up a city with a city.

Step 73

Back up a culture with a culture.

When a network group starts to grow and someone starts to make money, the word spreads. If the group starts in an office or a company, the word will spread to all of the employees. If it starts in a church or a mosque or a synagogue, soon everyone else in the group knows about it. Maybe you will recruit a veteran in the police force or the army and he or she will get all of their buddies involved.

There is nothing wrong with that. In fact, it can be the secret to quick growth. But once again, this important principle kicks in. You must keep the network moving. You cannot get stuck in one apartment or one city and you cannot get stuck in one culture. Do everything you can to take full advantage of the foothold you have but keep looking for ways to spread to new groups of people.

One of my best friends brought home the power of this principle in a big way. He emigrated from Hungary to Australia and eventually built businesses all over the world. He started building a Network Marketing business in Sydney and soon found his way into the Hungarian ethnic community there. When his company went to Hungary he went back with them.

He learned another lesson along the way. It is better to work in groups of three. If one goes into a new market alone their success rate plummets. Two are better but three are substantially better.

After several failures, eventually using this formula, he had success in Hungary. He followed the model in Finland and Poland and Czech Republic and Slovakia and Slovenia.

Once you catch on to this principle you can employ it elsewhere. Look for a large church, mosque or synagogue or a large corporation that employs large numbers of people. Try to sponsor three and watch it take off within the group.

At some point you will reach saturation, a dirty word for network marketers. Sometimes the leaders of the company or neighborhood will feel threatened by your business enterprise. Sometimes the religious leaders will feel that the people are being distracted. So get into a culture but back it up, too. Back up a culture with a culture.

Step 74

Back up a country with a country.

Ultimately, as your business grows, you will want to have networks in other countries, too. If an economic or political crisis hits one country, you will have a back up source of income in another.

There is another principle behind backing up a group, a city and a country. As the upline mentor you are the source of communication. And if you stay positive and share the best of what is happening in each group, that is, if you practice the principle, "Pass negative upline, pass positive downline," you will be able to use the good news from one region to inspire the other.

Fear and doubt, the great enemies of Network Marketing, will be vanquished.

Step 75

Spend less than you make.

This may seem like an insult to your intelligence. It is a principle of financial planning, not Network Marketing. Of course you should spend less than you make. But most great network leaders make a point to talk about it because there is the temptation in this business to start spending to keep up with your growing reputation.

Some people will equate the numbers of distributors in your group to your income. That is usually a mistake. Most groups have one very large leg and that is usually pass-up income. While it is important to show success, don't feel under any pressure to spend money just to impress other people. Be patient, your success will be real.

Step 76

Don't quit your job too quickly.

One of the reasons some people take up Network Marketing is to be able to walk away from an onerous job. They may hate the hours they work or the bosses who control them or the toil on their health.

Don't be too quick to quit. This advice comes from thousands of networking leaders in dozens and dozens of countries around the world. Can you learn from someone else's experience? Many people before you have seen quick growth and decided that working full time would only speed up the process. With some rare exceptions they found the opposite. Their networking business grew faster when they were working a job.

I am not sure why this happens. Maybe it has to do with routine and discipline or motivation. And maybe when you have a job you are circulating and meeting new people. Whatever the reasons, you should not ignore the advice and experience of so many.

Step 77

Keep out of debt and don't let your downline run up a big debt.

The purpose of building a network is to create the income to make dreams come true. And not just your dreams but the dreams of people you love. But even a good income does not guarantee success. You must know how to manage the money that comes your way.

Here is a basic principle passed on to you from the greatest networkers in the world: Don't get too deeply in debt. Pay your bills. And don't let your downline run up a big debt, either.

There are several reasons why this can get out of hand. One is greed. Your downline paints a picture of what they can do and how it will build your network. They order hundreds of CD's which you pay for. They promise they will pay. But when the time comes there is no money. Their plans didn't work out. And you are left with the debt.

Don't worry, they say, we have another chance to pay it all back, we are planning another event and this one will work. They show you the details and now you want your money back so you go along with it. What was once a small debt becomes a big one.

Stop the process immediately. It will never end. You are not going to get your money back. You are not a bank. Quit lending money. You are a networker and if you manage money poorly it will duplicate down through your group and they will all be suffering as a result.

Step 78

Invest in yourself.

For a networker, the best investment you can make is in yourself. You will always have your name. If you put money into promoting yourself, your network will benefit from it.

You can hire a ghostwriter to write a book about your ideas. You can hire artists to build a website. You can produce CD's that teach the lessons you have learned.

Your new product not only helps you, it helps your group. You now become a name that can be used to prospect and to recruit. You will soon have more credibility to teach others and speed up the process of building your network.

No matter what happens to your network, your name and the money you invested in it will still have power.

Step 79

Keep a check on your vital signs.

If you are a patient in a hospital they will monitor your vital signs. This includes your heartbeat and your blood pressure. They can learn a lot from any sudden changes.

Likewise your network has vital signs that will give you a warning when you need to work it harder or differently.

There will come a time when your network is so large and scattered that you cannot get enough personal feedback to know what's going on. And sometimes the anecdotal feedback is misleading.

There are several ways to track the growth of your network. Obviously you want to keep track of the products you are moving, the sales volume and your level in the company. You can track the number of CD's they are moving through the group and the numbers that are attending functions.

But your goals and the company's goals are not always the same. You are trying to build a network that will be ongoing regardless of circumstance.

For a networker, the best investment you can make is in yourself. You will always have your name. If you put money into promoting yourself, your network will benefit from it.

Step 80

Understand the economic whiplash, or the six month delay.

There is a basic principle of economy that is sometimes referred to as the whiplash. You can see the whip moving toward you and then you hear its crack but the sting of its touch comes late after you think it has done its work.

This is very true in business cycles.

You may watch on television as the commentators and the pundits talk about a failing economy. You may even see the stock markets plunging. But when you visit the shops they are full of people. The restaurants are busy. It seems as if the economic downturn is a figment of the media's imagination. And then it begins to hit. You hear of people losing their jobs. There are home foreclosures and bank defaults. Finally, you begin to read and hear reports of a comeback. The economy is on the mend.

And that's when you feel the pain as the whip catches you and you suffer financial setback.

There is a delay between what you do in Network Marketing and the reward for your labor. Be patient, it takes time for all of your work to register and result in appreciable income.

When building a networking business you may be inconsistent and work hard for a few months and then get discouraged because of insufficient profit. And yet, even when your work stops, it can be resilient. Or you jump back in and go to work only to see your network wane and drop back in spite of your best efforts.

This happens because of the delayed reaction between what you are doing or not doing and the results it produced. Some networking leaders believe that there is a six month delay between what you do and the results you will get in building a network.

Knowing this will transform your work. A year of fairly consistent work is required to get the momentum needed to build a network. Most of the success will come in the last months of that year when the network doubles month by month.

So here's the good news of the whiplash principle. When you work and get a network going and you start making phone calls and you stir up activity and you feel no positive sting, don't despair. You will only see the movement of the whip and later the crack and the report online of what you've done. The real sting, the positive sting, the money that comes from what you have done, is in the whiplash after.

The point is we have to be cracking that whip and cracking that whip and don't stop. Don't wait for the money, just get your network going and keep it going. Get the money coming in. There is a delay between what you do and what you see and what you work for and the result you begin to realize. Understand that and you won't panic.

Step 81

Be patient, some things take time.

Sometimes, not very often, but sometimes, a distributor is doing all the right things and still sees no growth. When things are not going well, stop and seek counsel from your upline mentor. Don't keep doing the wrong things. Don't go into denial. Be willing to see that there is no growth and make corrections.

When you are launching a new group you wouldn't want a distributor to waste a list of prospects. If he or she is not successfully recruiting from their list, you should stop them and recalibrate. When your network reaches into the thousands of distributors and your CD's and planned events are not growing, you must be willing to do the same. Don't keep doing things that aren't working. Don't panic. But stop and recalibrate.

Having established that point, there are times when you are doing the right thing and it doesn't work because it isn't enough of the right thing. Some strategies take time to work. And some take a greater emphasis to be effective. This is a basic reality of any strategy whether it be in sports or war or politics or business.

When you have counseled and consulted and you have determined that you are right on course, don't panic. Be patient. Give your network some time to respond.

Step 82

Be flexible.

Great generals are sometimes known for the orders they break, not the ones they keep. No one can follow all the steps in this book. Everyone makes mistakes or takes a wrong step. These are not rules that bind you. The marketplace changes, government rules change, companies and products change. And sometimes when that happens, the steps to success change, too.

Don't become legalistic about building your network.

My first sponsor into Network Marketing, Dexter Yager, was a legend and very wealthy and successful. This meant that he was often on the road and unavailable. It meant that I often had to talk to his wife, Birdie Yager. And she was a great example of flexibility.

When I was sponsored our company had no starter kits available. They were backordered. Our emerging network complained. "How can we build a business without kits?"

I met a man at the grocery store and was shocked to see that he had a notebook with the name of our company on it. You mean someone else in my own hometown belongs to this company? How can that be? The opportunity has already passed this way. Why should I even try?

Having met the man at random, we started talking. "How many do you have in your network?," he asked.

"Twenty."

"And how long have you been in?"

"About a month."

"Not bad," he said. "And what is your favorite product?"

"Well," I admitted, "We haven't gotten any of the products yet, they are all backordered."

"Well," he answered, "You should have gotten some products in your starter kit."

"We don't have starter kits, either," I said. "They are backordered, too."

He was shocked. "What? You don't have starter kits? Well, did you sign an application?"

"Not yet."

"Then you aren't in. You don't have twenty. You have nothing. You are not even in the business yourself yet."

I was very upset by this news and immediately called Birdie Yager who calmed me down. "Kits are overrated", she said. "You're growing. Just keep doing what you're doing. When people get kits they get out all the products and start asking questions and spend all their time on paperwork. It slows you down."

I called my group together and told all of the complainers that Birdie Yager said we were just fine. In fact, it's better this way. The Yager's are millionaires in networking, they know what they are dong.

Then one day, weeks later, the trucks pulled into our neighborhood and started unloading the kits. Because we had been so desperate for product some of us had ordered extras. And, sure enough, the phone lines were buzzing with questions about product and the paperwork.

I called Birdie in a panic. "We've got kits now and everything you said is happening. Things are a mess."

"Well, what's wrong with kits?" she asked.

"Well, you told me it was better to build without kids. You said that the people would be distracted with questions about the paperwork and the product and all hell has broken loose here and I don't know what to tell them."

"Ohhh," Birdie said knowingly. "I see. Well, tell me. How many people are in your group now?"

"Thirty."

"Okay," Birdie said, "Time for kits. If you are at thirty it is perfectly acceptable for you to get into the products and the paperwork. That won't slow you down that much and you have to eventually do it. Now that you are thirty, the timing is just perfect."

I called our group together and reassured them all. We are right on schedule. Everything is fine. We are now a network of thirty. We should now start getting our paperwork going and learn all about the products.

It is likely that I have embellished this story a bit. It happened a long time ago. We may have had some products and kits at the beginning, but the spirit of the story is accurate. Birdie Yager never panicked. She adjusted to the situation. It was great without kits, it was great with kits.

Be flexible.

Step 83

Give your distributors everything they need to know to be successful.

You don't tell your kids everything but you do tell them everything they need to know. Likewise, you don't need to tell your distributors everything. But you do need to tell them everything they need to know to be successful in Network Marketing.

A common mistake of networkers is to judge their downline by their own situation. If the leader is struggling with money and can't afford to go to a function, he or she will assume that it is likewise too expensive for their group. But if the function will help your network grow, tell them about it. Promote it. Don't limit the growth of your network by your own experience. Tell your people the truth and let them decide what they are going to do about it.

While you don't tell your network many personal things, neither does your network tell you everything. They don't always report their lost investments or when they inherit money from a relative who died. So if you just make a habit of giving them what they need to know to be successful, then they can decide how to respond.

Some leaders fear the naiveté or innocence of their distributors. They feel a responsibility for keeping them from doing too much or spending too much. They may say to themselves, "This distributor is in serious financial trouble so I'm not going to tell them about this program or this convention. It is for their own good, they need to save their money."

But you're not God. You are their upline. It is not your job to decide their future for them. It is not your power to decide whether or not they will be successful or what level they will reach. Let them decide. Give them the information they need.

You may say, "Well, I just want to provide a little balance. They need to know both sides of the argument."

That's the problem. There is no balance. They have already heard a lot of reasons why they shouldn't go to the weekend seminar. They didn't need you to tell them. Their spouse, their neighbors, their parents, all told them to stay home. That argument was covered. You say, "We want a little balance, it's not all about money, it's not about greed."

But you are the only person on earth to tell them why they need to go. Don't blow it. That's your job. Other people will tell them to stay home. Other people will tell them that they are wasting their time and wasting their money, that they will never be successful in networking. Your job is to believe in them, to tell them why to go. If they were worth sponsoring in the first place, then they deserve to know the truth, and if the truth is that they should be attending the weekend seminar, then your duty is to tell them.

Step 84

Keep in mind you are in a business, not a charity.

One of the reasons I launched a Network Marketing business was to be able to have the money and time to devote to charity. It has worked. Over the years I have been able to raise a lot of money and help start a number of worthy charities including the Charity Awards which has been hosted in the White House and has honored some of our world's greatest leaders. And I have played a modest role in the beginnings of Mercy Corps which has distributed $2 billion in food and medicine around the world.

But networking is not a charity. And if you treat it as such, it will not grow and duplicate and it will not provide you with the income that will allow you to do charitable work.

After speaking at a conference in Bali, a poor worker came to the front of the room to meet me. He heard what I was saying about the importance of business CD's and why you should listen to them to pick up the experience of others. Now while others around him were wearing suits and dress clothes, the worker was dressed in poor, dirty clothing. His hands were callused. He was very skinny. He was wearing very light cloth slippers as his shoes.

He said, "I hear what you are saying about CD's but they cost me almost a month's wage. What can I do?"

We talked a little about how he could borrow CD's from others and pool his funds to buy them with a group and other such ideas.

But I was deeply saddened by the experience and outraged. Who had sponsored this man? He had no money. Were they taking advantage of him and his ignorance? What chance did he have to succeed?

I felt like saying to him, "Get out of Network Marketing. This is not for you. Save your money. Work as hard as you can and use your money to feed your children and your family and yourself."

I wanted to take him home and put his children through college and buy him a little house, that's what I wanted to do. I was heartbroken.

But let me tell you the reality. This was a man who digs ditches for a living and puts his kids to bed hungry every night. That man's children will grow up and they will dig ditches and put their kids to bed hungry every night. He and his descendants will live in slums. They will always be hungry. They will always die young. Nothing will change unless someone in his family gets a CD or a book or a person who can teach them something new and different, something that will awaken their mind and change the paradigm. Someday, someone, will have to break through the barrier or they're destined to dig ditches in perpetuity.

Give your people the truth. Don't forget the balance; you're the upline and if you don't believe in them, nobody believes in them. If you don't think they can be successful in life they have no hope. For some, you're their only hope. If you believe your CD can change their life, give them a future and give them a hope. Believe they have the ability and they are just as smart as anybody else. If they have the right information, then they have a chance. If you don't believe that, then they don't have a chance.

And don't make your business a charity because it will duplicate. If you give away the CD's you are giving away your distributor's chance to make a living and have an income.

My encounter with this man haunted me for some time. And then I realized if he is in an endless cycle, so am I. We are all trapped at our own level of knowledge and income. And it will take a shock for us to break out of it.

Step 85

Remember, what gets rewarded, gets duplicated.

What you reward becomes self-replicating; it duplicates. What you ignore eventually dies.

If you reward weakness in Network Marketing it will spread and duplicate throughout your group. If you have a distributor who whines, always complaining about you and your team and the company and the CD's and the events, and you try to placate that distributor by meeting with them and rewarding them with stage time or dinner at a restaurant or little notes in the mail, then you will soon have a large organization of whiners. The problem will not be arrested, rather it will spread.

If you reward negative people, trying to cheer them up, you will see negativity duplicate throughout the group. What you reward, you grow. And that includes the bad as well as the good.

If you give attention to distributors who owe you money hoping that they will change their habits and pay you back, you will soon have a group of people who owe you money.

Of course, you want your negative people to become positive. You want your doubters to become believers. You want the people who are hurt to become healed and whole. But, as you will see in the next step, the way you accomplish that in networking is exactly the opposite of how you would respond as a parent or a leader in society.

Step 86

Work with your strongest group.

In a family, parents will work with the child who has the greatest need. Sometimes it will change as the child grows older and the parents' time and direction will move to a sibling. And in society, we will move with compassion to the person with the greatest need helping them get on their feet again.

Network Marketing doesn't work that way. In Network Marketing you work with the strongest distributor in the strongest group under the strongest mentor until that group and those leaders are earning substantial amounts of money and are completely self sufficient.

Why is that?

Because, as was pointed out in the last step, what you reward becomes self replicating; it duplicates. What you ignore eventually dies.

If you have a distributor who is a self starter, who is always on time, who pays their bills and who requires no attention at all, you may be saying to yourself, "This distributor is low maintenance. I don't have to work with them at all." But that is exactly the person you should work with and promote and honor. That is the person you should be talking to on the telephone and bringing into your confidence. What gets rewarded, duplicates. Reward strength and you will get a strong network of people who pay their bills and do what they promise.

Step 87

Do a business review with your downline.

One of the greatest teachers in Network Marketing is a second generation MLM'er named Jody Victor. Jody came into my group for a weekend and taught us all how to do "a business review." The "business review" is now a standard process in Network 21 and other great Network Marketing systems although the methods differ.

Now this gets a little hard to explain but I will give it a try. Jody arranged for me to meet alone with him and each one of my leaders, one by one. In these sessions we asked each distributor to set a six month goal. Where would they like to be? At what level in their business? And then we broke the process down into months. What would they have to do the first month to reach the goal and then the second month?

After we established these goals, we brought back the leaders one by one and went through their downline leaders in the same fashion. Almost never did Jody or I interrupt. We asked questions and let them answer. A few times, if the distributor set a goal that was unreasonably low, we would question why but usually we let them talk.

The results are astounding. Almost always the distributor has higher goals that you would recommend or imagine. When you ask, "Well, how are you going to do that?", they will come back with some piece of new information you didn't know about them and new information about their contacts and their plans.

Most surprising of all, the numbers start adding up quickly. If the lowest person in the network does even a fraction of the work they are envisioning, then the uplines will be pushed over the top easily, one by one, and in quick time. If everybody does even a little, the growth will be spectacular.

This is an exercise that is both good and bad.

It is bad to realize that most distributors in Network Marketing are not working at all. They are doing nothing. They have sponsored others and are bluffing, pretending to work, encouraging others to get busy.

But it is good to realize that only a little bit of work can make a difference, and if all in a group decide to do a little at the same time, it can lead to explosive growth that in turn leads to more growth.

Step 88

Learn to be an effective counselor.

You will very quickly learn that the problem with building a network has nothing to do with the logic or eloquence of your presentation, nor is it about the money in the company's compensation plan. It isn't about the products, either.

The reason your distributor is not building his or her group is because they are facing a problem that has nothing to do with Network Marketing. They are getting a divorce. Or their daughter is anorexic. Or their son is addicted to drugs or computer games. Or they have lost their job. They are in the middle of a lawsuit with their own parents.

It is not about you. It is about them.

Now you didn't sign on to be a marriage counselor or a psychiatrist but you will find that people are self destructive, ridden with guilt and remorse, egotistical and selfish, lazy, impulsive. There are reasons why they haven't succeeded financially. And those reasons will raise their ugly head when they try to succeed in Network Marketing.

It is not your job to dictate their life. But it is your job to listen. To sit and listen to their problems and offer them support and hope and objective opinions when it is necessary.

Remember that you are almost a parent figure even if they are older in years. You are now the upline mentor. They just need to know that you care about them and you understand their pain. Sometimes that is enough to get them moving.

Your instincts will be to move on to another person. But I can tell you from personal experience that you will find the same thing with someone new. Problems are endemic to human nature. And no matter how self assured their exterior, when you get to really know someone, the problems will come tumbling out.

Keep this in mind. To be successful in Network Marketing you don't have to solve all of these problems and neither do they. I have been with thousands of Network Marketing leaders and they too have divorces, daughters who are anorexic and sons who are addicted to computer games. The difference is not that one has problems and the other doesn't. The difference is that one sponsored people and the other didn't. Stay focused on what you have to do to become successful in networking and hold their hand when they are hurting.

Step 89

Respect the opposite sex.

I once went to a private dinner with one of the greatest European Network Marketing leaders in the world. When I asked him to list his top ten most important principles in networking, he started rattling off the familiar things. Get a dream. Listen to positive CD's. But when he got down to number seven he caught me by surprise. He said, "Never counsel a member of the opposite sex without someone else in the room."

Now this was Europe, not the United States where litigation is so prevalent. So I asked him to explain himself. And why this principle, even if it had merit, ranked so high on his list.

He told me how entire groups with thousands of distributors were lost in months by scandals among the leaders.

Now, we all have emotional and physical needs. There is nothing wrong with that. And some people find their soul mates for life in Network Marketing. But if you want to build a network that provides you with an income without ceiling, and an income that is ongoing and secure for life, then you better learn to separate your personal, private life from your public, networking life or you will see everything you have worked for ruined before your eyes.

Leaders should teach couples to respect each other.

Sometimes an upline leader will gain the admiration of downline distributors who in turn become disillusioned with their marriage partner. "Why can't my husband be a big dreamer like him?"

A good leader will teach both the husband and the wife to nurture each other and build each other up and encourage each other. A good leader will not denigrate a husband or wife in front of the other.

And yes, as the network giant taught me, don't put yourself in a vulnerable situation. "Never counsel a member of the opposite sex without someone else in the room."

Step 90

Never make a recommendation until you have heard both sides of a dispute.

There will be times as an upline mentor when you will be called to arbitrate a business dispute in your growing network. Don't look for these moments because they are not going to endear you to your distributors. If your resolution is fair, it will probably be hated by both sides and viewed by both as a mistake. But sometimes not making a decision is like leaving a splinter in the body. It will lead to an infection that is far more dangerous and painful than removing the splinter.

The first step, and the most important step, is to listen thoroughly to both sides. Don't talk, except to ask questions. Get them talking, first alone with you. Their words will sometimes provide the answers on how to best resolve a difference.

And later, when you have assurances that they are willing to talk to each other, bring them together.

Step 91

Keep your upline mentor informed. There should be no surprises.

It is pretty useless to have an upline mentor if they don't know what's going on. A computer only crunches the numbers you input. Even good advisers can only offer opinions based on the facts you give them.

No one can be objective about themselves. It is why presidents and kings have teams of people to advise them. And you, too, need help in building your network. You need someone else who benefits from your success, who can offer perspective.

Keep your upline informed.

Now, we have discussed that there are exceptions. There are parents who will kill their own children. And there are uplines who will hurt you even if it hurts themselves and their own income. But once you have established trust and you are reasonably certain that the upline mentor with whom you are working will offer sound advice, then make sure they know the troubles that are brewing before they become out of control.

Step 92

Always defer counseling and recognition to the higher leader.

Always defer to the higher leader. This is not about ego. This is about business. Remember, what gets rewarded, gets duplicated. If you treat a higher leader with deference and respect, then your group will strive to achieve that higher level themselves.

The higher leader should get preferential seating in a restaurant and at a convention. If you are traveling together, give the leader the best seat. Don't dominate the discussion. Ask questions of the higher leader. It is pretty stupid for you to be talking about the lessons you have learned from your thousands when they can be talking about lessons learned from tens of thousands.

Never counsel a downline in the presence of a higher leader. Ask their opinion. But make sure they are privately briefed and know the situation so they don't inadvertently cause more harm than good.

At a public gathering, always introduce the highest leaders, say their names and give them public recognition for their achievement.

This works well regardless of the popularity or talent of the upline leaders. If the person is obnoxious, prideful, crude, it will only affirm to your network that if such a person can build a big network, they can surely do it themselves.

Of course, as we have discussed, there are exceptions. If a higher leader arrives uninvited and unapproved by your upline mentor, you may make exceptions. I have been at events where very high level leaders sat without introduction to the audience. And they understood. It was not their organization. They had not been invited to speak or teach. They had asked to come to audit and learn from the event and their host graciously allowed them to do so. The upline mentor, leader of the host group, made the decision. They are producing the event and thus taking the financial risk involved.

Sometimes a higher leader will show up for predatory purposes. They want to sell their program or even build relationships with your downline and get them to transfer to their group. Do not automatically honor a higher pin. If they are people of integrity they will not surprise you without talking with your upline mentor. And if they do accidently surprise you, they will not expect you to recognize them.

Step 93

Reward numbers as well as level of achievement.

Not only should you honor and defer to the higher leader, you should likewise show recognition to the distributors in your group who organize the most people. Who in your group distributes the most CD's? Who buys the most tickets for events or brings the most people to the conventions you promote? These people should be rewarded even if they have not reached the higher levels in the company hierarchy. Remember, what gets rewarded, gets duplicated. And the secret to your growth is the successful education and inspiration of your network.

So you promote the distributor with the higher achievement so that others will see and believe that it is possible to succeed in your company. But you also promote the person who is the most successful at supporting your teaching and training program because that is the key to your growth. The first is an example of achievement. The second is an example of how to get there.

The first may have reached a higher level and even have a greater income but still may be unable to command large groups of people because other downline leaders have taken charge and are building the groups. There is nothing wrong with that. That is a level that most networkers want to reach. Sometimes these leaders are in retirement or semi-retirement. Their job is to travel and spread goodwill and inspire new distributors with their story.

The second person is using your formula for building a network and they are involving people. Their work gives them a moral authority that may transcend their current level and income in your business. But if you want them to keep working, then you need to honor their work. And if you do, it will duplicate and create other leaders who will bring even more people to your events and use the CD's you are promoting.

If you are hosting an event and one of your distributors downline successfully promotes it and brings half of the people, then that leader should be honored. And if you have trained them and know what they teach, they should be given the option of sharing from stage.

Why should a leader who is not supportive of your seminar and who brings no distributors and provides no money to help pay the bills be given a prominent place in your program? Why should they be the expert, the hero, to people in the audience who were recruited by someone else?

If they are loyal to you, then the person who brings the people should also get the recognition. They should stand on stage before their own people in the audience. Other leaders are watching. If they want to speak, if they want recognition, they know what to do and they know how to get it. If they promote your event and bring people, they too will be honored.

This principle applies at the highest levels of network building. It has led to events with 100,000 distributors in outdoor coliseums.

Step 94

Use healthy competition to build your network.

One of Solomon's more controversial tenets declares that "envy is the motivation of life."

There is nothing that can build a network faster than healthy competition. And there is nothing that can tear it apart more quickly than a fight between rival distributors. Obviously, you want the "healthy competition."

The key is to have distributors who are close to the same level and a level playing field. Three are better than two. There should be no favoritism and you should make it clear that any competition is only to help motivate because, unlike a race, in this contest everyone who crosses the finish line gets a gold medal. The object is to succeed and build an ongoing, substantial retirement income, not beat out a rival who you didn't even know existed before you launched your network.

You are the audience. They will work for your attention. And they will work harder if they see that you are monitoring their performance and cheering them on.

You will remember the role that momentum plays in building a network. Most big groups had explosive periods. And most fast growth occurs when there are competing groups.

Step 95

Don't prejudge prospects or leaders.

One of the greatest leaders in networking once lived in abject poverty. He and his wife had no toilet in their apartment. They had to share that at the end of the hall. Once a week they visited the modest home of their parents and used their shower to bathe. And yet I sat down with American presidents and this man. He had no education, no credibility, a poor vocabulary and yet he built one of the largest networks in the world. Even today, people in his downline fill soccer stadiums and coliseums around the world.

Another of the world's greatest networkers with an even larger following internationally with a two billion dollar business in Japan, started out as a highly paid engineer. He and his wife were graduates of a prestigious university. They have lived in classy homes and driven beautiful automobiles. They are well dressed, smart and well organized.

And then there is the top Network Marketing earner in the world and a dear friend of mine. He was a surfer, a beach bum who smoked marijuana without much ambition at all.

The point is that you cannot prejudge who will be successful and who won't. Sometimes it is the man or woman in the shadows, the one who is overlooked, who will surprise you.

When I wrote *The Raising of a President* I noticed that often there was an ambitious parent, either the mother or father, and they would tend to focus on one of the children, often the firstborn. All of their dreams and wishes would be directed to this child, but they were almost always disappointed.

When Augustine Washington lay dying in Virginia, his whole focus was on his firstborn son, Lawrence Washington. Lawrence was given the estate at Mt. Vernon. Lawrence was given all the training in the iron works and the complete education in England. Now, there was a backup son who was also given an education in England but the younger son, George Washington, was given nothing. He received no education at all. He was way down the list.

It's very interesting to follow the genealogy of the Washington family. After America won its independence and General George Washington became president of the new American States, the British nobility concluded that there had to be some noble blood in his family somewhere. How else could this Washington fellow have beaten them? So they ran their own genealogical studies to chart the family of this American upstart and finally they presented them to George Washington.

He turned them down. He said, "I'm not interested in where my ancestors came from or who they were. Here in America we decide our own destinies. It's not decided by our ancestors and our blood."

Even so, these studies make for good reading. When you trace back the history of the Washington family, you find these people 500 years ago doing and saying some of the same things that the Washington's were doing and saying in Virginia years later.

The Washington family was not nobility, not even minor nobility. They worked really hard on their land and they carefully brokered their marriages trying to climb the social latter. The father would buy as much land as possible but he needed lots of sons to run the farm to make it profitable, and when he died the land had to be split up again. The firstborn would get the larger share, but this process was tedious and it took years for the Washington family to ratchet up their position in English society.

With hard work, many land purchases and clever marriages, the Washington's were eventually on the cusp of nobility when Oliver Cromwell came to power. Anyone associated with King Charles I and the Royal Family was now cast out.

So the Washington family left for the New World and the Virginia Colony. When they arrived they found that even Virginia was taken. As primitive as life was in the New World, there was a strict hierarchy with fifteen families that dominated society. There was no room for the Washington's.

George Washington, the future president, was an eleven year old boy when he stood at his father's death bed. All of the attention was on the firstborn son, Lawrence. But a few years after the death of the father Augustine, Lawrence Washington died as well. It was the overlooked little boy in the shadows who changed history.

There is this same re-occurring story throughout the American presidents. You see it in modern times. When World War Two began in 1939, Dwight Eisenhower was only a major on staff with General Douglas MacArthur in the Pacific. The big shot in the family was Milton. He was Director of Information at the Department of Agriculture. When the Eisenhower's came back to Kansas for family Thanksgiving, they'd sit around the table and listen to

Milton's stories of life in Washington, D.C. He would tell stories of White House receptions and what President Hoover and President Roosevelt had said. He was the rising star. But in just a few years Dwight Eisenhower became Commander of the Allied Forces and shortly after was elected President of the United States.

There's a scene in my book where old Joe Kennedy is in a car in the early morning with a friend. It's cold outside and they are watching Joe's son, Jack Kennedy, standing outside a factory gate shaking hands with workers. The younger Kennedy was campaigning for Congress.

"I never thought I'd see this in a million years," Joe said to his buddy. "I always thought that Jack was too sick and too shy."

The Kennedy's had always expected the firstborn, Joe Kennedy, Jr. to run for office and eventually be president. But young Joe died in a World War Two bombing raid. "Never in a million years did I think it would be Jack," said the father. "I didn't think he had it in him."

This, too, is a story of biblical dimensions. The prophet Samuel meets Jesse's sons expecting to anoint one of them as the new King of Israel.

"I can't understand it," he says to Jesse. "But I know it isn't any of these young men. Do you have any other sons?"

"No," Jesse says. And then he remembers. "Well, there is David, the youngest. He is out tending the sheep."

"Go get him," says Samuel. "He must be the one."

It's a marvelous story. You can't judge a person by their looks or their age or their education. Don't write people off. Don't decide who the nobility is, who will succeed and who won't.

Right now, somewhere in the shadows, there is an eleven year old boy who will one day be president. And no one knows who he is. He may not even believe in himself at this point. Likewise, you don't know which of your prospects and which of your leaders are going to break from the pack and build a mammoth network that will make dreams come true.

Don't judge too quickly.

Step 96

Be a good broker and learn to sponsor wholesale.

The way some people make money during economic downturns is through brokering. Brokers make money because property is sold and property is purchased and deals are made whether dealing with land or art or stock certificates. It doesn't matter if the price is high or low, the broker gets a small commission on each transaction so the broker does well when there is activity.

Essentially, when we are talking about brokering, we are talking about helping to bring people together. Finding someone who wants something and introducing them to someone else who has it. This, too, is how large amounts of money are made in Network Marketing, by simply bringing people and networks together. A classic illustration from business history is Aristotle Onassis. At one time he was among the richest men in the world. He conceived of the idea of building large oil tankers, larger than any ships that had ever been built before. He met with engineers to find out if it was possible. Most of them said, "No, that's impossible, that's outrageous." "It's dangerous." "It's too costly. Even if they could be built, the use and maintenance of such ships would be impractical. They would have to be constantly busy to justify their cost and the oil business is cyclical." "Big is good but too big is bad."

Onassis kept shopping until he found engineers who said theoretically, at least, it could be done. Armed with this information he went to his business contacts in Saudi Arabia. He essentially proposed to them a hypothetical question: If I guarantee that this much oil can be shipped in this amount of time, in this amount of volume, could I be given a reasonable exclusive? The answer came back that yes, theoretically, he could have such an exclusive. But as far as they could see, moving oil in that volume in such a short period of time would not be possible.

And then he went to the investment bankers: If I can get an exclusive from the Saudi's, and if I can deliver this amount of barrels of oil in this amount of time, in these ships, would you finance the project?

Now, of course I am simplifying a very complicated story that involved many years and thousands of pages of paper. But this illustrates what he did on a much more sophisticated scale ratcheting up his project with each visit to the bankers, to the engineers and to the Saudi's. Eventually he put together that deal. He found the engineers who built the ships that had never been built before. And he signed an exclusive contract with the Saudi's guaranteeing a certain volume of barrels of oil to be transferred and he got the money from other investors to pay for the whole thing.

Aristotle Onassis was the broker and he didn't use his money to finance the project. Afterward, a number of books were written about OPM – other people's money. But the principle is a sound one.

Some of the most successful networkers in the world have learned how to broker deals, some bringing entire networks together, some even bringing networking companies together. This is called wholesale prospecting and networking. Instead of prospecting a single person, you are prospecting companies and sometimes non-competitive, non-MLM networks or groups of people, helping them achieve their goals by matching them up to your company. It only takes a couple of these transactions to create a substantial income for life. Think big. When the opportunity presents itself, be a wholesale broker.

Step 97

Stay focused.

There's a puzzling story in the Old Testament about Jacob and Laban. Jacob had to work to get his bride from his father-in-law, Laban. Both men were shepherds and the father-in-law decided to help Jacob out a little bit. He said, "We will both tend the flocks and when there are newborns, I'll take the white sheep and you can have the spotted sheep."

So in this story, Jacob takes a brown stake and carved off the bark so there are white spots on the brown stake, and he hammers it into the ground near the riverbank where the sheep go drink. Well, as the story goes, when they have their offspring there were large numbers of spotted sheep. What was going on? The genes, the genetic code for the spotted sheep or the white sheep, were already in place. So why did more of them become spotted?

The implication is that when they went down to drink the water, they saw the reflection of this spotted stake in the ground.

They saw the spots, so they were thinking spots.

It's an ancient story, thousands of years old but the message is that how we picture ourselves, how we see ourselves, what we focus on, that's what we will become.

It's very easy to become distracted in Network Marketing. One can become consumed by the politics in the company, or passionate about a change in policy or in product, or in what country will be opened next. But in the end, your income is dependent on what you do. Not what the company does. It is the phone calls you make next Tuesday that will determine your income. Stay focused on the things that YOU can do to make your business successful.

Now, it is true, in any company and any market, there are times of transition and upheaval and there are times when you must be willing to make strategic decisions about your loyalties, but conditions are never perfect.

Once more I quote from Solomon: "If you wait for perfect conditions you will never get anything done." The greatest networkers stay focused.

While the world around them rages and debates, they keep making calls and speaking to friends and earning their monthly paycheck. Don't let the problems around you become your excuse for failing to do your own work. Ultimately, you cannot control what others do, but you can control what you do. Stay focused.

Step 98

Loyal leaders come through relationships.

As your network grows larger you will need leaders to assume more and more responsibility for running your business. Unfortunately, there is no shortcut for this. If you find a capable manager or promoter and give them responsibility but fail to take the time to maintain a personal relationship, you will be only creating a competitor. They may eventually cause more harm than good.

The problem is time. You do not have time to juggle dozens and dozens of relationships. This is why you must create systems. But even the most efficient system cannot replace the loyalty that comes from a personal relationship. You must decide who your leaders will be and you must carve out time for them.

Step 99

Make a decision.

Your success in networking, as in the case of your success in life, will require a decision. Once you make the decision that you are going to reach a certain level, the numbers and ideas and even the prospects will start to come.

I had a cousin who announced as a young boy that he was going to be a stamp collector. And I watched over the years as the relatives and friends started to send him stamps. "Why did he get them? Why not me?" It has nothing to do with favoritism. It had to do with his decision and the stamps started flowing his way.

In 2005 I wrote a book entitled *The Raising of a President.* It was about the parents of the American presidents and the early life of their successful children. Some of the stories are rather shocking. I didn't find what I thought I was going to find.

The parents of the American presidents came off as abusive and possessive and just as crazy as anyone else's moms and dads. There was really nothing special about them. Franklin Roosevelt's mother refused to let him take a bath without her until he was nine years old.

Abraham Lincoln's father was a very ignorant man. He would knock his son to the ground with his fists. He had heard rumors that maybe Abe Lincoln wasn't really his son and so he hated him and favored a step-son. He saw Abe as lazy because Abe would read a book while he, the father, was plowing a field.

But there was something very liberating in this study. I found that even though the president's experienced abuse and neglect and the same experiences that many other children have, they rose above it and achieved great things.

This was a liberating experience for me. I realized that I am not a prisoner of my childhood experiences. I am not limited by something my father or mother said to me or did to me. I am free to become whatever I want to become. If Abraham Lincoln can become one of the greatest presidents in American history, and his dad would hit him with his fists so hard it would knock him to the ground, what can I become? It was a decision away.

When I reached my first significant level in networking I decided I was finished. It wasn't for me. It was too much work and not the kind I enjoyed. But when I attended the weekend retreat and I listened to all of the other speakers, I began to think about the next level. What would it take? How would I do it? How long would it be? The answers surprised me. It was within reach. I made a conscious decision and the next year arrived at the next level. I did this for consecutive years and marveled at the power of making a decision.

When we see pictures of Abraham Lincoln we usually see the silhouetted president in the window of the White House. But when Lincoln looked into the mirror, what did he see? He most likely saw the little kid living in a cabin in the woods of Indiana, miles from the nearest neighbor. He was in the White House a little more than four years but he lived in that cabin for fourteen years. That was the longest period of his life in one place. Lincoln's experience of isolation and ignorance and loneliness and poverty was far worse than most of us. His mother used thorns instead of buttons to hold her clothes together. The buttons were too expensive. And yet Lincoln became one of the greatest figures of American history.

The point is that you can become whatever you want to become. Who do you want to be? Who do you see in the mirror? The Proverbs say, "As a man thinks in his heart, so is he."

Ninety-Nine Steps to Network Marketing Success

1 - The importance of a dream.
2 - Share your dream with people you love.
3- Get counsel before you do anything in the business.
4- Listen to 5 recommended CDs.
5- Make a list of prospects.
6- Double your list of prospects.
7- Team up with someone else.
8- Practice setting up meetings with your prospects and your team.
9- Promote your upline team.
10- Don't call all of your prospects at once.
11- If involving a married couple, invite both the husband and wife.
12- Get into a Network Marketing educational system.
13- Read positive books.
14- Practice showing the plan.
15- Get some friends to see you rehearse the showing of the plan.
16- Audit other presentations.
17- Start a meeting in your own home.
18- Get the meeting out of your home.
19- Get a new face into your group.
20- Make sure the new face is loyal to you.

21- Have someone else introduce you at the meeting.
22- Develop your own signature.
23- Listen to a positive CD before showing the plan.
24- Have your upline teach your downline what they need to know.
25- Look successful.
26- Learn how to do one-on-ones.
27- Give a prospect a unique reason to get into your business.
28- Sponsor your weakness.
29- Calibrate your prospecting approach.
30- Sponsor peer and above.
31- Teach all of the networking principles, not just the ones that work for you.
32- Learn to teach how to lead rather than how to build.
33- Know when to take charge.
34- Follow up within the first 48 hours and never wait more than three days.
35- Use your products.
36- Talk about your products.
37- Categorize your new distributors as business builders or product people.
38- Revisit distributors in the business-product categories.
39- Never let a prospect get away without a referral.
40- Help your new distributor make a list.
41- Rehearse the invitation with your new distributor.

42- Remember, you are responsible for everything.
43- Set long term and short term goals.
44- Develop good work habits.
45- Get into a good field-oriented educational system.
46- Think of CD's as your employees, put them to work.
47- Build a CD library.
48- Lead by example.
49- Go to the functions.
50- Promote the functions.
51- Take your distributors with you to the functions.
52- Understand the dangers of crosslining.
53- Pass negative upline. Pass positive downline.
54- When you have no upline mentor, create one yourself.
55- Remember, people will work for recognition or money.
56- Promote your system.
57- Help your downline set networking goals.
58- Teach your downline how to promote.
59- Teach others how to promote you.
60- It's not what your upline does for you that will make you rich, but rather, what you do for your upline.
61- Understanding the importance of momentum.
62- Keep in mind that it is hard to build more than three separate groups at the same time.

63- Sponsor fifteen to twenty to find your three.
64- Don't decide on leaders too quickly.
65- Get help in launching an out of town group.
66- Make your prospect build locally before launching an out of town group.
67- Plan on making four weekly trips to launch an out of town group.
68- Plan on making a monthly trip for one year.
69- Visit your large groups at least once a year.
70- Back up a distributor with a distributor.
71- Back up a leader with a leader.
72- Back up a city with a city.
73- Back up a culture with a culture.
74- Back up a country with a country.
75- Spend less than you make.
76- Don't quit your job too quickly.
77- Keep out of debt and don't let your downline run up a big debt.
78- Invest in yourself.
79- Keep a check on your vital signs.
80- Understand the economic whiplash, or the six month delay.
81- Be patient, some things take time.
82- Be flexible.
83- Give your distributors everything they need to know to be successful.
84- Keep in mind you are in a business, not a charity.

85- Remember, what gets rewarded, gets duplicated.
86- Work with your strongest group.
87- Do a business review with your downline.
88- Learn to be an effective counselor.
89- Respect the opposite sex.
90- Never make a recommendation until you have heard both sides of a dispute.
91- Keep your upline mentor informed. There should be no surprises.
92- Always defer counseling and recognition to the higher leader.
93- Reward numbers as well as level of achievement.
94- Use healthy competition to build your network.
95- Don't prejudge prospects or leaders.
96- Be a good broker and learn to sponsor wholesale.
97- Stay focused.
98- Loyal leaders come through relationships.
99- Make a decision.

Made in the USA
Lexington, KY
28 September 2012